LORD,
I NEED TO HEAR
YOUR VOICE

Freedom from What Holds You Captive:
From Despair to Hope

A Bible Study for Women

DR. PATRICIA ALLISON

CROSSBOOKS

Crossbooks™
A Division of LifeWay
1663 Liberty Drive
Bloomington, IN 47403
www.crossbooks.com
Phone: 1-866-879-0502

Cover Image Credit: Kim Sanders-Manees

First published by CrossBooks 7/15/2013

ISBN: 978-1-4627-2951-7 (sc)
ISBN: 978-1-4627-2952-4 (e)

Library of Congress Control Number: 2013912053

Printed in the United States of America.

This book is printed on acid-free paper.

ACKNOWLEDGMENTS

This book would never have happened without God's holy guidance in my work with women living in crisis. He has blessed me richly by introducing me to women who are seeking freedom from what holds them captive. I was introduced to the Table Rock Freedom Center, Branson, Missouri, in 2008 when I first met Kim Sanders-Manees. Kim has a heart for women who are held in bondage by life controlling choices of which have lead them down a path of self destruction. As Director of TRFC, Kim graciously allowed me to volunteer my time to teach a course on personality preferences, lead Chapel meetings, fill in administrative duties as needed, and be a prayer partner with her and with each student. This experience was no accident. God fully revealed His plan for me to live a life in His service, as a mentor and friend to women at the Table Rock Freedom Center. I am so honored to have served Him in this way. The beauty of the experience then led me to have a heart for women everywhere who are facing daily trials and trauma due to harmful habits and unhealthy choices. These choices have had a significant negative impact on the women and their families, causing a need for change that can only be found through following God's plan for their lives.

In addition to my time at the Table Rock Freedom Center, I was blessed to have been given an opportunity to begin a support group for women at a local church. These women were living with daily challenges of destructive life controlling choices, such as alcoholism, drug addiction, eating disorders, and other unhealthy life styles. Each woman involved in my support group was seeking God's purpose in their lives while trying to balance motherhood, relationship problems, and surviving on a low income. I want to thank the First Baptist Church, Hollister, Missouri, for allowing these women to meet with me weekly at the church. It has been an uplifting experience to share with church leaders and members who have a heart for all of God's people.

My husband, Larry Allison, has been my biggest fan and greatest encourager. He has always helped me reach my dreams and has stood by me as my tears flowed during times of discouragement and fatigue and also cheered me on during the moments of personal victory. He has always affirmed my passion for working with women in crisis and has never doubted God's calling in my life. Living with and loving a Godly man is one of the greatest gifts God has given to me.

TABLE OF CONTENTS

CHAPTER 1

Hearing God's Voice:
Is God Calling you to Lead?

If it is serving, let him serve; if it is teaching, let him teach; If it is encouraging, let him encourage; if it is contributing to the needs of others, let him give generously; if it is leadership, let him govern diligently; if it is showing mercy, let him do it cheerfully. Romans 12:7-8

If you are reading this book it may mean you have decided to move closer to God and away from self-destructive behaviors. It may mean you are ready to seek God first in all things. Perhaps you are looking for a resource to use to help you lead a group of women in crisis. Whatever your reason, it is my prayer that this book will help you grow in the work of Christ and find your purpose for doing His work. God has given me a passion to work with women who are in need of unconditional love; women who crave relationships with safe people who will not judge them for the lives they are leading or have led but rather help them to see life through new eyes, the eyes of Christ. We have no way of knowing what lies in the heart of another and are we not called to assume intentions but to love and accept, as Christ loves and accepts us. These women are people who have often been cast aside by those they love most, whether by a spouse, child, parent, or friend. God has placed upon my heart the task of creating curricula that can help women find personal peace through understanding God's purpose in their lives. Each chapter can be studied in isolation or as part of a weekly Bible study with each chapter building on the previous chapter in a systemic approach. However, each chapter may also be studied as an individual Bible study if so desired.

As the idea for this book was planted in my heart I kept thinking about the story of the Samaritan woman taken from the book of John, chapter 4. This woman was a cultural outcast and someone who had made poor choices in her personal decisions. She had a past and was not living a righteous life. Jesus met her at the well where she was drawing water. Through her conversation with Him it became evident that He already knew everything she had ever done, even those things of which she was not proud. Jesus offered her *living water* if she would follow Him. He was showing the woman that although her life was in disarray, she could accept His offer to know Him and accept a life of redemption through understanding and following Christ's loving purpose. This story led me to entitle the group of women I work with as "Women at the Well" since Jesus already knows everything we have done and still offers us living water (John 4:10).

I have spent most of my adult life as a teacher and leader in the educational system among families living in the inner city. Having struggled with family issues as a child, I felt called to work with children living in similar circumstances and certainly found many opportunities to help families in crisis. I have spent countless hours reading and researching God's message through prayer,

Bible study, and collecting notebooks full of information gathered from sermons given by those I admire and know to be led by God, both in local churches and from world-renowned pastors. I have always enjoyed writing but I never thought God would call me to help Him reach hurting women by developing a teaching method that would make a difference in the lives of these women. I have been awakened in the night with hurting women on my mind; I have not even met these women, but somehow I can see their faces and feel their pain. I have tried to convince myself, and yes, even God, that He has called the wrong person. I have tried to explain to myself and to God that I am far too busy to write a book and that I will be happy to continue to do what I do in His name, but I cannot possibly find the time or talent to create a book. And yet, the women I work with have affirmed my efforts and those who know me well have continually encouraged me to step up and share my knowledge and experience with others. I know now that God has called me to be His messenger through a burning passion placed within my heart. That passion is for serving those who are held captive by personal choices that have led them to unhealthy living conditions. When God calls us to work for Him, He does not give up, but rather may send others to help us recognize that we are chosen to be His servants. After all, as my pastor explained, "it is not about what we want; it is about what God wants" (Hal Schrader, personal communication, April 7, 2013). The Scripture that speaks loudly to me regarding my call to serve is found in Matthew 20:27, where Jesus was explaining to the disciples the importance of being a servant leader by doing for others rather than expecting to be served. In the study section assigned to this Scripture, The Life Application Bible, NKJV, states,

> Jesus described leadership from a new perspective. Instead of using people, we are to serve them. Jesus'

> mission was to serve others and to give his life away. A real leader has a servant's heart. Servant leaders appreciate others' worth and realize that they're not above any job. If you see something that needs to be done, don't wait to be asked. Take the initiative and do it like a faithful servant. (p. 1722)

This Scripture explanation has revealed in part why Jesus had to die: to be ransomed. His death would *redeem all people from the bondage of sin and death*. Because of the sacrifice of Jesus, we can understand a need to continue His work and to help others find the freedom of which He speaks. In verse 28 Jesus said, "just as the Son of Man did not come to be served, but to serve, and to give His life a ransom for many." This particular verse was revealed to me during my personal Bible study and I feel it was by no accident, but rather God's way of *hammering home* that which He was calling me to do.

Called by God

> I thank Christ Jesus our Lord, who has given me strength, that he considered me faithful, appointing me to his service. 1 Timothy 1:12

As Christians we are called to serve others by showing them God's ultimate plan of salvation. As I continued to study the Scripture and learned more about Christ as a servant to others, I felt God was making it evident that He was asking me to create a curriculum and share it with others so that greater numbers of women could receive the help needed to remove them from the bondage of Satan's grip. It is my prayer that this book will be used to reach many more women than I can do alone. And now here it is. I am a firm believer that God uses ordinary people to spread His message and does not call us to do any task for which He does not provide the tools. "And God is able to make all grace abound to you, so that in all things at all times, having all that you need, you will abound in every good work" (2 Corinthians 9:8). "For it is God who works in you to will and to act according to his good purpose" (Philippians 2:13). It is my prayer that you will find this book to be a helpful resource to you as you work with women who are seeking God's peace and purpose in their lives or as you feel a need to find God's voice for yourself.

Be a Disciple

> "If you hold to my teaching, you are really my disciples." John 8:31b

Helping others to find Christ is a glorious example of how God uses His people to present His message. Ask yourself if you are able to put others before yourself in a way that offers unconditional love, provides encouragement and support, and presents honest and humble service to those in need regardless of what that need may be. In Galatians, we learn how the spirit of God (fruit of the spirit) provides traits that are evident in us when we emulate God's love for others. By knowing Christ and understanding His nature and relationship with us, we are given characteristics that imitate His love for others and we are asked to use those characteristics to make a difference in the lives of those we encounter daily. "But the fruit of the Spirit is love, joy, peace, patience, kindness, goodness, faithfulness, gentleness, and self-control" (Galatians 5:22).

Note the Great Commission found in Matthew when Jesus sent His disciples out to disciple others: "Therefore go and make disciples of all nations, baptizing them in the name of the Father and of the Son and of the Holy Spirit, and teaching them to obey everything I have commanded you. And surely I am with you always, to the very end of the age" (Matthew 28:19-20). Read also John 20:19-22 to discover Christ's message to His disciples upon His return from the cross: "Peace be with you! As the Father has sent me, I am sending you. Receive the Holy Spirit. If you forgive anyone his sins, they are forgiven; if you do not forgive them, they are not forgiven" (John 20:21-22).

Mother Teresa at one time stated, "We can only do small things with great love." This statement allows us to understand that God does not expect all of us to be Billy Grahams but rather to do what we can do where He has called us to be. Not only should we pray that people come to Christ through the work of His disciples but we are each called to be one of those disciples by our willingness to serve others by offering respect, honor, love, and grace as God does for us. We are called to teach others to be Christ-followers in addition to Christ-believers.

Jesus passed His work on to his followers to spread the truth in salvation. If God is asking you to do this work then understand that your authority comes from God and that Jesus has shown, through His service to others, how the work must be carried on. In John 20:23, we read that Jesus has given a spirit-filled power, as a guide for them to go out among the people and deliver the good news of Jesus, and how their sins can be forgiven as a result of His death on the cross. Therefore, pray for those who will come to faith through those who serve as disciples of Christ. Be one of those disciples.

Search Your Heart

> Test me, O Lord, and try me, examine my heart and
> my mind. Psalm 26:2

How do you know God is calling you to serve others through Him? I would suggest the following steps to find your passion for what God is calling you to do:

1. Use daily prayer and ask God to reveal how you may serve Him. Remember, answers to prayer may not always come instantaneously. God's timing belongs only to Him and we are to be obedient as we wait on Him. Be genuine in your heart as you pray about serving. Read I Thessalonians 4:1, "Finally, brothers, we instructed you how to live in order to please God, as in fact you are living. Now we ask you and urge you in the Lord Jesus to do this more and more."

2. Recognize that God's voice can come as an impression on your heart, something that seems to keep resurfacing in different circumstances. Listen to your heart. Think about Philippians 1:9, "This is my prayer: that your love may abound more and more in knowledge and depth of insight."

3. Determine if what you are feeling is really from God by asking yourself if it feels right. Does what you feel line up Scripturally? Look at Romans 12:2, "Do not conform any longer to the pattern of this world, but be transformed by the renewing of your mind. Then you will be able to test and approve what God's will is—his good, pleasing and perfect will."

4. Seek council from those who know you well, including your pastor. Ask others what they see as your gifts and talents. Ask yourself if what you are feeling matches with

what others suggest as your gifts. Review the Scriptures on spiritual gifts paying close attention to Romans 12:6, "We have different gifts, according to the grace given us." Sometimes others see areas in us of which we had no idea we were gifted.

5. When you think about what you feel God is calling you to do, does it give you a feeling of excitement or dread? If you do not sense excitement then perhaps it is not what God is asking you to do. He wants us involved in things of which we are suited and things we enjoy doing. Reflect on John 15:10-11, "If you obey my commands, you will remain in my love, just as I have obeyed my Father's commands and remain in His love. I have told you this so that my joy may be in you and that your joy may be complete."

6. Finally, recognize your passion and determine if the feeling is so distinct that you know the feeling is coming from God. Things will fall into place if you continue to ask God for His revelation first and then follow His guide. Step out in faith and do the work He has called you to do. Consider Revelations 17:14, "They will make war against the Lamb, but the Lamb will overcome them because He is Lord of lords and King of kings—and with him will be his called, chosen and faithful followers."

Prayer

Dear Lord Jesus, I come to You today with an open heart and a request for wisdom as You call me to serve others on behalf of the kingdom. Help me to fully understand what You are calling me to do and to do that which You have called with a willing spirit. Remind me daily, Lord, that I am Your servant and am here to bring Your message to those who are facing a life in the wilderness. Provide the gift of discernment upon my own spirit so that I help and do no harm to those who are seeking Your voice. Allow me, Oh, Lord, to be a witness to those who are hurting and afraid by giving to them the hope in You that is your gift to all who are searching for inner peace and healing. In Your name I humbly pray, Amen.

Conclusion

Not everyone is called to work with women who have chosen unhealthy life styles. However, we are all called to be like Christ and this may mean doing something in His name that is difficult. We are all called by our spiritual gifts that God has designed in us and we must all be willing to use those gifts for His glory. It may mean moving out of your comfort zone and taking on something you thought you would never see yourself doing. I challenge you to pray about how God can use you to reach the needs of others. We are not all called to do great things but we are all called to do something, no matter how small, to make God more evident to those around us. Should you choose to work with women who are living in crisis situations, it is my prayer that this book will help you find a path to guide them in hearing God's voice while understanding His purpose for each of them. It is about being purposeful in doing what God has called you to do: Commitment to discipleship through obedience to Him.

CHAPTER 2

Be God's Voice:
Will you answer the Call?

Note: This chapter prepares leaders to address the concerns that may be encountered when working with women searching for God's voice and His purpose for their lives.

> "Set an example for the believers in speech, in life, in love, in faith and in purity. Until I come, devote yourself to the public reading of Scripture, to preaching and to teaching." 1 Timothy 4:12-13

The above Scripture is representative of Paul's work with Timothy and was offered at a time when Timothy needed some encouragement. This is not unlike today with those individuals God places in our paths. It is not uncommon for women living with turmoil and dysfunction in their lives to feel depressed and unaccepted by friends and family members. For some individuals, the idea of changing old habits and taking a *leap of faith* is so overwhelming that a successful conclusion to needed life change does not seem possible. The Bible teaches us to reach out to those in need of encouragement and support. The Life Application Study Bible provides sound advice for leaders working with people who could benefit from encouragement as they work toward making life-altering change.

(1) Begin with encouragement. People who know we will encourage them will be happy to work with us. (2) Expect of others only what you expect of yourself. People will resist being held to unfair standards. (3) Develop expectations of others with consideration for their skills, maturity, and experience. People will reject or fail to meet expectations that do not fit them. Be patient with distracted or slow learners. (4) Monitor your expectations of others. Changing circumstances sometimes require revised or reduced expectations. (5) Clarify your expectations with others. People are not likely to hit a target that no one has identified. (6) End with encouragement. People love to be thanked for a job well done. (2005, NIV, p. 2040)

I heard someone tell my husband that they felt God has given me a great gift . . . the gift of gab. I did not know whether to be insulted or to admit full agreement. I have been known to speak up, ask the hard questions, and provide a comment on most any subject. However, I also pride myself in basing my questions and comments on finding truth. I want to learn as much as I can about where and how God wants me to serve in His name. Part of my ability to speak Bible-based truth is also because I am willing to listen to those who have much more wisdom than I have and who are more schooled in the Biblical literature. As I mentioned in the introduction, I have been given many opportunities to work with women living in crisis, which has served as great teaching for me. Because of God's blessing upon my life and His gift of allowing me to meet and work with so many wonderful women who struggle each day to find their way through personal loss, fear, and tragedy, it has become apparent that God is asking me to be His voice; delivering His message of love and redemption to His children. I have no doubt that I am doing exactly what He has called me to do and I am honored to help others find that same path.

The following outline is designed to walk you through a process of reflection as you begin to focus your attention on how and when to lead women in crisis. Use this outline for some self-talk along with your own Bible study as a means to build confidence in the work God has called you to do in His name.

a. Recognize the passion God has placed in your heart to help others by doing His work. Follow the gentle nudges that come from God's wisdom. He does not place you in a position to lead unless He is there to guide your heart. Max Lucado wrote,

> There are certain things you can do that no one else can . . . There are things that only you can do, and you are alive to do them. In the great orchestra we call life, you have an instrument and a song, and you owe it to God to play them both sublimely. (1998, p. 55)

b. Be willing to recognize the difference between your will and God's will. Turn to trusted friends who know you well to help you discern if God is calling you to lead a group of women who are in need of His presence in their lives.

c. Why do this? It is not ours to question the plan God has for His people. If we are called to lead then do what you can to prepare yourself for the work according to His purpose. Pray fervently for understanding and wisdom by committing yourself to prayer asking God to reveal His plan to you.

d. Be a servant leader as Christ served others and begin by deciding your real purpose behind leading a group. Consider this calling as a means to serve others and to walk with them in the journey of discovery. Part of having a servant's heart is being open and honest with others so that you may hear what they have to say while also sharing what you believe, as found through biblical principle. "Brothers, if someone is caught in a sin, you who are spiritual should restore him gently . . . Carry each other's burdens, and in this way you will fulfill the law of Christ" (Galatians 6:1a-2).

e. Become the hands and feet of Jesus; Become His voice through your actions. Through your servant leadership you can extend the kingdom of God through people by being a spiritual risk-taker and spreading the seed of truth through Christ, even though not all truth will take root. God has a plan to use us for demonstrating what He is already doing. We are the picture on the wall, the map to the destination, the hand held out to lift up and walk beside. In Matthew 10 we are reminded that we should give generously to others of our time, love, and possessions. Additionally, Matthew 5:16 states "Let your light shine before men, that they may see your good deeds and praise your Father in heaven." In this passage Jesus is reminding us to be the *reflection of Christ* (Pastor Griswold, personal communication, June 27, 2012) and to be a beacon of truth—do not shut your light off from the rest of the world.

f. Understand that Jesus taught us that helping others is a priority. An example of this principle is found in Luke

13 when Jesus became frustrated after healing a crippled woman on the Sabbath. Healing was considered a doctor's job; a form of work that should not occur on the Sabbath, therefore Jesus was criticized for healing the woman on this revered day. When Jesus saw others being critical to this service He rebuked them by reminding them that they were willing to care for an animal on this day but not willing to rejoice at the healing of a woman's suffering from Satan's bondage. For our purpose, this story explains the importance of relieving the pain of others when we are called, regardless of the situation.

Skills and Attributes

> Each one should use whatever gift he has received to serve others, faithfully administering God's grace in its various forms. 1 Peter 4:10

Understand that you do not need a PhD in biblical counseling nor do you need to attend seminary in order to have the skills needed to help others find the path to God's kingdom. God does provide you with what you need if He has called you to do the work. Be willing to ask God to give you wisdom to discern the need that is present among those who have been sent to you. "I am your servant, give me discernment that I may understand your statutes" (Psalm 119:125). He will walk with you as you find your voice to share God's love for His people. You may feel you do not have the right words to bring God to light, but He will become the light within you and guide your voice to speak truth to those who need to hear it most. Pray for His guidance in all things.

God tells us to avoid judging others (I Corinthians 5: 12,13) in fact He expects us to emulate His loving heart by accepting anyone who is in pain by loving them unconditionally. We are not called to point fingers and find fault; we are called to support and encourage. This does not mean you should avoid speaking truth but rather, as His follower, share the good news of His love for all people. Speak truth in love, even when the message is difficult to hear. Use the Scripture to guide your approach because it is about helping rather than judging. "Therefore judge nothing before the appointed time; wait till the Lord comes. He will bring to light what is hidden in darkness and will expose the motives of men's hearts. At that time each will receive his praise from God" (I Corinthians 4: 5). Do not advise, but rather guide: Listen with your heart. "Administer true justice; show mercy and compassion to one another, do not oppress the widow or the fatherless, the alien or the poor. In your hearts do not think evil of each other" (Zechariah 7:9-10).

Be a compassionate listener by using attentive body language through eye contact, affirm others by nodding your head, and slightly lean toward the speaker to show you are listening. Sit together without a table or other obstacle separating you if possible. If the program is to be used as a study program, have a table and comfortable chairs available. You do not need to be a professional counselor to listen to the hurting soul of another. Being available and attentive is enough to show someone that you care and that you are willing to hear the pain they need to share. To support another person, it is often necessary to allow time for processing before they are able to verbalize their pain or concern. Be patient and supportive as feelings are revealed.

You may find yourself listening to words of complaint or anger, but to listen without interruption shows you care about their feelings.

When a person feels you care enough to listen attentively and with interest, they are more likely to relax and begin to share more freely. Once they feel it is safe to be open and honest, they will then be more willing to listen to what you have to say in return. Open your heart as well as your ears. And when it is time to speak, speak the truth with love and patience. Paul wrote, "Preach the Word; be prepared in season and out of season; correct, rebuke and encourage—with great patience and careful instruction" (2 Timothy 4:2).

Realize that you do not need to have all of the answers. You do not need to jump in and solve the problem. Use God's Word to help the individual search out personal truth. Introduce them to the concept of obedience as a means of preparing for crisis. Such as, consider understanding God's plan for us as a means to feel His support during the bad times as well as the good times. In Jeremiah 29:13, God promises us that we will seek Him and find Him when we seek Him with all our hearts. The search involves being committed to the journey and to be obedient to His will. Consider serving through showing respect of the person, honoring their right to feel what has been placed on their heart, demonstrate uncompromised love for them as a child of Christ, and offer grace and understanding. To serve others is to discover the image of God within those you work with and in turn help them to discover that image in themselves.

Be aware that diversity will play a part in how you lead. All of us look at life in different ways. How you view the Scripture may not coincide with the understanding of those who are or are not schooled in biblical principles. God made each of us unique and we will each perceive God's voice in different ways. Some authors refer to this as a *spiritual pathway* and consider it as "the way we most naturally sense God's presence and experience spiritual growth" (Ortberg, 2005, p. 121). Become cognizant of the differences among the women you will encounter and their personal perceptions of God in their lives.

Be a Role Model

> Be imitators of God, therefore, as dearly loved children and live a life of love, just as Christ loved us and gave himself up for us as a fragrant offering and sacrifice to God. Ephesians 5:1-2

Paul is a prime example of modeling Christ's behaviors. In I Corinthians Paul is explaining to the Corinthians that they should follow Him as a leader, not because he was the perfect example, but because he had spent a great deal of time with God, in word, and in prayer. Paul was fully aware of God's presence in his life at all times and served as an example showing others that they, too, could follow God by leading in the same way. Paul was able to help others understand that they could note the parts of Paul's life that emulated Christ and then also model their own lives after that of Christ. Paul said in his letters to the Corinthians; "Therefore I urge you to imitate me. For this reason I am sending to you Timothy, my son whom I love, who is faithful in the Lord. He will remind you of my way of life in Christ Jesus, which agrees with what I teach everywhere in every church" (1 Corinthians 4:16).

As you begin to model God's love for each person, consider the following:

a. Be willing to share your own story. Although you may not have experienced addiction or abuse in person, you may want to share how you can relate. Be honest if you have not gone through any thing like the person you are supporting. However, if you have something that you can share that would be helpful in relationship, it is good to be as open as you are comfortable.

b. If you want the ladies in your group to be on time for group and to show up each week, then be committed yourself to do likewise. Use the old adage of *walk the walk* as well as *talk the talk*.

c. Remember, the ladies you work with will be watching you. Some will have trust issues and will watch closely to see if you, like so many others, will turn against them. However, most will become very trusting and loving toward you and will want to have what you have when they see God's love shine through you. It is not uncommon for them to emulate how you behave and relate to others, even when you do not realize they are watching you.

d. Always follow through with your plans and/or promises. This will take patience on your part because women living with life-altering issues are often insecure in their belief and unsure that they can change and be accepted by you or by God. Be completely humble and gentle; be patient, bearing with one another in love (Ephesians 3:2).

e. Be willing to follow up with those in the program. There will come a time, for a variety of reasons, that someone will leave the program. Some will move away, some will find other programs (i.e. residential programs, jail time), or some may just decide they do not need the help. The reason does not matter, however it does matter that you do not give up on them and follow through in the best way that you can. An example was when one of my ladies had committed a crime and was sentenced to seven years in prison. The prison was located in a different state from where I was working and living. I decided I would not give up on her and at the time of this writing am still sending her books, letters, and visiting in person when I am in the state where the women's prison is located. She is learning that I meant what I said in our group when I promised not to give up on her. I am merely showing her what God does for us; He never gives up nor does He stop loving us.

Be Aware of the Issues

Then he turned to his disciples and said privately, "Blessed are the eyes that see what you see. For I tell you that many prophets and kings wanted to see what you see but did not see it, and to hear what you hear but did not hear it." Luke 10:23-24

You may find that women in crisis have developed a lack of accountability and also demonstrate entitlement behaviors. Such behaviors are often products of addiction, childhood trauma, childhood parenting issues, or any psychological experience that causes one to develop inappropriate or tainted views of the world. Additionally, you will always find some women who suffer from very low self-esteem. They do not feel worthy of forgiveness, love, or acceptance. Your job is to help where and when you can. As stated earlier, never place judgment, but accept those women who God has brought to you as His children of whom He loves completely. You will find that some women will insist that they are unlovable, that God could never forgive them for all that they have done or for the choices they have made. This is not an uncommon feeling among those who have fallen into sinful choices or self-destructive behaviors. "We feel unworthy based on the sense of our own sin" (Dr. Jeremiah, 2012, p. 203).

The following list does not encompass all of the possible dysfunctions of women you will encounter, however the list does give you a starting point of understanding for the most common debilitating behaviors of which I have found to be evident in so many women. Although much of the information covers addictions, there are other behavioral issues discussed throughout the book that affect the way women relate to God and to others. I encourage you to seek information from credible sources as you work to understand the causes of some addictions, the characteristics that will be evident, and loving words to comfort and guide those wishing to change bad habits or personal problems through the love of Jesus Christ. Ultimately, you will want to help others experience spiritual growth. Shapiro (2010) describes spiritual growth as "an ever-deepening capacity to embrace life with justice, compassion, curiosity, awe, wonder, serenity, and humility" (p. xiii). Perhaps the best way to experience spiritual growth completely is through the work of God in our lives. Help others develop a mind set for seeking God's plan for their lives and to discover what He created them to be. Encourage each person to embrace truth, hold on to faith, and continue to seek understanding.

Harmful Habits and Addictions

They promise them freedom, while they themselves are slaves of depravity—for a man is a slave to whatever has mastered him. If they have escaped the corruption of the world by knowing our Lord and Savior Jesus

Christ and are again entangled in it and overcome, they are worse off at the end than they were at the beginning. 2 Peter 2:19-20

For the purpose of this next section, I have included working definitions for *habits* and *addictions* to better facilitate mutual understanding:

> "Habits are learned patterns of behavior or attitudes repeated so often they become typical of a person" (Hunt, 2011, p. 24).

> "Addictions are a compulsive, enslaving dependence on something, resulting in detrimental patterns of thinking and behaving. There are *substance addictions* (e.g. alcohol, tobacco, heroin, inhalants) and *process addictions* (e.g. gambling, eating, shopping, sex)" (Hunt, 2011, p. 25).

People suffering from any kind of addiction or harmful habit, can be helped over time, but there is no *quick fix* to help someone addicted to a substance that alters their view of the world. When an altered view of what is considered *normal* is part of a person's daily existence, it becomes confusing, and possibly painful, as the individual learns a new way of thinking and behaving. Because the altered view often results in changed, and/or destructive, behaviors, your ability to remain focused will be necessary to best support the individual. To work successfully with someone struggling with addictions takes patience, belief that God can save the addict, and a willingness to be consistent in purposeful love for the person while speaking truth against the behavior.

In 2 Peter 2:19 we learn that whatever can enslave us has mastered us. The Life Application Study Bible explains:

> A person is a slave to whatever controls him or her. Many believe that freedom means doing anything we want. But no one is ever completely free in that sense. If we refuse to follow God, we will follow our own sinful desires and become enslaved to what our bodies want. If we submit our lives to Christ, he will free us from slavery to sin. Christ frees us to serve Him, a freedom that results in our ultimate good. (NIV, 2005, p. 2115)

However, we know that most addictions can be conquered when correct treatment is sought. As a servant to God, leading others to Him is a good beginning. Help the person who is controlled by harmful substances to find God's voice through you. Be the example of His love through your support and understanding. You may find yourself asking the enslaved individual to be open, honest, and willing to share troubling or difficult examples of harmful behaviors. It will be easier for them to open up to you if you can be open yourself about your own struggles and experiences that have caused you to run or turn away from God. As the leader, it is important for you to examine your own spiritual health and work on your intimate connection with God, asking Him to guide your thoughts, actions, and words as you represent Him to those who are trying to find His voice for themselves. Be willing to seek out contacts for professional help offered through reputable organizations so that you may be a resource to the addict should they need intervention beyond what you are able to offer. Hunt wrote, "No single approach to breaking addictions is ever enough because bondage is multifaceted, and thus deliverance must incorporate numerous approaches. All addictions involve not only the body, but also the heart and soul of those they hold captive" (2011, p. 184).

The following Scriptures may be used to address the area of habits and addictions:

- Many will follow their shameful ways and will bring the way of truth into disrepute. 2 Peter 2:2
- Be very careful, then, how you live—not as unwise but as wise, making the most of every opportunity, because the days are evil. Ephesians 5:15-16
- No servant can serve two masters. Either he will hate the one and love the other, or he will be devoted to the one and despise the other. Luke 16:13
- There is a way that seems right to a man, but in the end it leads to death. Proverbs 14:12
- Everything is permissible for me—but I will not be mastered by anything. 1 Corinthians 6:12
- Search me, O God, and know my heart; test me and know my anxious thoughts. See if there is any offensive way in me, and lead me in the way everlasting. Psalm 139:23-24
- No discipline seems pleasant at the time, but painful. Later on, however, it produces a harvest of righteousness and peace for those who have been trained by it. Hebrew 12:11

Symptoms of Addictive Behaviors

Who has woe? Who has sorrow? Who has strife? Who has complaints? Who has needless bruises? Who has bloodshot eyes? Those who linger over wine, who go

> to sample bowls of mixed wine . . . In the end it bites
> like a snake and poisons like a viper. Your eyes will
> see strange sights and your mind imagine confusing
> things. Proverbs 23:29-30,32-33

Addicts tend to have a propensity for avoiding the truth. They may try to convince you that they are not really addicts, but rather just caught up on using drugs or alcohol recreationally and that they are able to stop whenever they wish. They will explain that the addiction is not even really an addiction, but something that does get in the way from time to time even though they are convinced they could quit at any time. Typical indicators of an addiction include:

- Drug tolerance—needing increasingly more of a substance to obtain the same effect.
- Physical dependence—suffering from chemical withdrawal symptoms such as nausea, sweating, shaking, and anxiety.
- Intense craving—developing a pattern of compulsive substance use.
- Loss of control—failing at attempts to decrease or stop the substance abuse.
- Targeting activities—choosing events only where alcohol or drugs are available.
- Continual substance abuse—continuing to use despite negative ramifications. (Hunt, 2011, p. 83)

You may find the addict is able to provide examples of people in their own lives (parent, sibling, cousin, friend, etc.) who really do have a problem while trying to convince you that they themselves are not anywhere nearly as involved as the person they are discussing. Part of this effort is about the fear of losing you as a supportive friend. They will believe if they are truly honest with you then you will turn away from them. They will, in turn, feel God could not possibly forgive them for the sins they have committed, therefore they will try to keep much of their experiences from you, at least in the beginning. We will discuss more about this in Chapter 5.

Providing excuses for the addictive behavior is commonplace among addicts and the level of excuses that will surface should not surprise you. When a woman makes the decision to attend your meetings/support group, you may witness some of the most creative explanations you can imagine as the individual tries to explain away the harmful behavior. Biblical Counselor, June Hunt, founder of Hope for the Heart, provided a compiled list of excuses given to justify living with an addiction or bad habit. I encourage you to read the following list and use it with your group to help them identify characteristics that speak to them personally.

- This makes me feel better; and besides, I deserve it.
- Lots of people do this; after all, no one is perfect.
- This habit is caused by my past. I really can't help it.
- It's useless to try to change or quit.
- I can control this anytime. I'll change when I'm ready.
- I don't want to try to quit and risk finding out I can't.
- Doing it one last time won't make any difference.
- What I'm doing is not really that bad. A lot of people do worse things.
- I've not been able to change before, so why try now?
- Everyone needs at least one vice.
- If I give this up, something worse will just take its place.
- This is not a good time for me to try to change.

- I don't have time to focus on this right now.
- As soon as I have a sign from God, I'll change.

Taken from <u>How to Defeat Harmful Habits</u> by June Hunt (2011), pp. 42-43.

Elements of Addictive Behavior

> My days are swifter than a runner; they fly away
> without a glimpse of joy. Job 10:25

Ultimately, you will find that those who show addictive behaviors often experience a very low self-esteem. This will be evident in many ways: body language, self-degrading language, hygiene, and energy level. The point is, these women will feel as though they do not matter to anyone, let alone God. Many of the women who have chosen drugs or alcohol to mask their pain have done so because they have been taught to believe they do not matter and therefore have no value. Why then would they feel God cares for them, when perhaps, their own parents did not regard them as valuable members of their family? I often share with my women that I personally do not believe there is such a thing as an accidental birth. Yes, I believe there are unplanned pregnancies, at least from our human viewpoint. However, if we were not to be born then God would not have allowed it. We were to be here because we know He has a plan for us and has since before our birth (Jeremiah 1:5). Additionally, we know we are so valuable to God that He sent His only son to die for us (John 3:16) and because He is even concerned with what happens to sparrows, He certainly holds higher value for His children (Matthew 10: 31). Remind the women; "Because God places such value on you,

you need never fear personal threats or difficult trials. These can't shake God's love or dislodge his Spirit from within you" (Life Application Study Bible, NIV, 2005, p. 1554).

Along with a low self-esteem, you may find women suffer from genuine fear. They may be living in fear due to financial concerns, living conditions, or fear that God has abandoned them. Fear can be a crippling emotion that leads to more use of alcohol or drugs to help mask the pain of fear. This is an area where you will want to instill upon the person living in fear that God does not leave us alone. He is within the reach of simply breathing His name. However, all too often we seek first our own means to solve whatever problem we face, instead of first calling upon God to help us discover His plan for us in all things. In the book What Women Fear, author Angie Smith (2011) wrote; "My prayer, and not just for myself, is that we will emerge as women who can say we trust our God fully and we are devoted to seeing Him in the midst of the fear" (p. 13). Although the plan is to follow God in all things, good and bad, we must remember that Satan is also out there pulling strings causing us to develop an inclination to draw upon our own will to solve the problem, instead of giving it over completely into the arms of God and waiting on Him. The following Scriptures may help you share the promise of God through His assurance that we need to be faithful as His love is faithful.

- For great is his love toward us, and the faithfulness of the Lord endures forever. Psalm 117:2
- Your kingdom is an everlasting kingdom, and your dominion endures through all generations. The Lord is faithful to all his promises and loving toward all he has made. Psalm 145:13

- Through love and faithfulness sin is atoned for; through the fear of the Lord a man avoids evil. Proverbs 16:6
- No temptation has seized you except what is common to man. And God is faithful; he will not let you be tempted beyond what you can bear. But when you are tempted, he will also provide a way out so that you can stand up under it. 1 Corinthians 10:13
- If we confess our sins, he is faithful and just and will forgive us our sins and purify us from all unrighteousness. 1 John 1:9

Types of Addictions

Although the following list will not address all forms of addictions, the information will give you an idea of the addictions often prevalent among women. The information has been researched and studied among women who have experienced one or more of those listed in this next section. I encourage you to read what you can find on any addiction of which you find yourself working with among the women you serve. However, it is important to note that if you are not a professional in any of these areas then it is wise to be willing to help the people you work with discover professional help when needed. Become aware of Christian counselors in your area. You may even wish to have information (brochures, etc.) on hand to share with those who appear to need clinical management.

> **Eating Disorders:** Body image (bulimia, anorexia, obesity) is a common problem, especially among women. As we are aware, our society places great importance on how women look physically. Body

image can relate directly to the self-worth of a woman who already struggles with acceptance from those she loves. June Hunt wrote a book entitled <u>How to Defeat Harmful Habits</u> (2011) and in her book she shares a vast amount of helpful information about various addictions, including that of eating disorders. I suggest you spend some time researching the effects of eating disorders if you find this is a concern among the women in your group. The following information is a brief overview of information provided by June Hunt in her book. There are other resources available regarding the concerns and hazards of eating disorders that you may wish to investigate.

Anorexia and Bulimia are common eating disorders that "are merely the surface symptoms of an underlying problem. Those suffering from these eating disorders have believed lies and have lost sight of the truth" (Hunt, 2011, p.169). Both disorders can have a profound effect on the physical health of an individual and may already have done permanent damage by the time they have entered into the group setting. Overeating that leads to obesity can be as damaging to the health of a woman as anorexia or bulimia and may lead to hypertension, diabetes, or heart disease. Unless you are a health care professional, it is not wise to try and diagnose an eating disorder in another person, but it may be necessary to intervene by sharing information on such disorders and encourage the individual to seek medical guidance. However, until the root cause of the disorder is addressed, the individual may decide to ignore your advice.

Substance Abuse: The working definition of substance abuse comes from the Baker Encyclopedia of Psychology (1985) and reads; "The use of a chemical—legal or illegal—to the extent that the usage causes physical, mental, or emotional harm." Although there are various chemical dependencies that lead to addictions, for the purpose of this book we will discuss drugs and alcohol in general terms. However, it is recommended that you seek more information on any type of substance abuse that may be evident in the lives of the women you work with so that you are able to make valid determinations and recommendations for any necessary outside help.

Drugs: A working definition for drugs comes from Hunt's work and reads, "Drugs are chemical substances introduced into the body that produce physical, emotional, or mental changes. Some drugs are helpful, and other drugs are harmful" (2011, p. 76). Unfortunately, some drugs prescribed to us by doctors for health benefits may also lead to addiction if not carefully managed. Be aware that drugs are taken in various forms: Ingesting, inhaling, injecting and include depressants, stimulants, hallucinogens, and narcotics (pp. 76-79). It would be of benefit for any leader who works with possible drug users to obtain a good resource for learning more about the signs and symptoms of drug abuse.

Alcoholism and Alcohol Abuse: Sadly, drinking alcoholic beverages is commonplace in many social events. It has become an accepted form of societal gatherings, especially for celebrations. Because of the accepted practice of drinking, it is possible for a person to acquire a habit, which can lead to serious health and safety concerns. When alcohol is used to either cause a euphoric feeling or used to avoid feeling badly about an issue, then it is likely a problem. According to Helpguide.org, "Alcoholism and alcohol abuse are due to many interconnected factors, including genetics, how you were raised, your social environment, and your emotional health" (para. 3). In Hunt's book, How to Defeat Harmful Habits, she explains that intoxication is the result of alcoholism or alcohol abuse and is described as follows, "Intoxication occurs when the influence of a substance in your body cause changes in your behavior, including mood changes, faulty judgment, slurred speech, poor coordination, unsteady gait, sexual impropriety, aggressive actions, and impaired social functioning" (p. 82).

To help leaders identify possible warning signs of substance abuse the following lists may be used as a guide.

Emotional Warning Signs:

- Anger
- Anxiety
- Depression
- Fear of rejection
- Frustration over little things
- Guilt—"My choices are bad"
- Shame—"I am bad"
- Unpredictable mood swings

Physical Warning Signs

- Bloodshot eyes
- Loss of sexual desire
- Night sweats
- Poor general health
- Shaky hands
- Skin breakouts
- Tendency to look older
- Unhealthy looking complexion
- Weight gain or puffiness

Behavioral Warning Signs

- Compulsive drug use
- Defensive about the addiction
- Denial that there is a problem
- Dishonest about usage
- Obstinate about change
- Rebellious toward those in authority
- Reclusive from those wanting to help
- Secretive about time spent on the addiction

Relational Warning Signs

- Associating primarily with other users
- Attempting to hide addictive behavior
- Being too weak to stop and too stubborn to get help
- Deceiving others about money spent on the addiction
- Lying to others about frequency of use
- Prioritizing the drug over people and profession
- Refusing to act responsibly in relationships
- Shifting blame to others for problems

Spiritual Warning Signs

- Aversion to Scripture
- Conviction by the Spirit
- Diminished prayer life
- Fear of God's punishment
- Feel estranged from God
- Hardened heart toward God
- Lack of joy
- Withdrawal from church life

Note: The above information was taken from How to Defeat Harmful Habits by June Hunt, 2011, pp. 87-89

It is necessary to be cognizant to the fact that women are held captive for many reasons. Although chemical addictions are common, you will find that sexual abuse is more common than we like to believe. Such abuse often leads to the use of chemicals or alcohol to help the victim mask the pain of the abuse, which in turn leads to a harmful addiction or life style. The following is a very brief overview of the effects of sexual abuse and it is recommended that should you find the need to understand the topic more thoroughly that you investigate through reputable sources.

Abuse (sexual, physical, emotional)

Women who have come from sexually abusive relationships at an early age may find intimacy difficult as an adult. If the symptoms from the abuse remain unresolved the victim may choose to live an alternative life style or develop substance abuse as a means to dull or remove the pain and unwarranted guilt created by the event. Lutzer's research on the Seven Snares of the Enemy: Breaking Free from the

<u>Devil's Grip</u> (2001) indicates, "the sexual identity of the [molested] child might be confused because the boundaries of protection have been violated" (p. 139). The author contends that once the child has experienced an inappropriate sexual bond, as created by sexual abuse, the child will seek to maintain that bond, regardless of how wrong it was. As an adult, the abused person continues to seek love and does not know how to find it normally or as God intended; thus, as an adult, often chooses a path of harmful or self-destructive behaviors that ultimately lead to negative consequences.

Although the above information discusses sexual abuse, the results of physical and/or emotional abuse have similar results. The child who is barraged with constant physical or emotional pain will come to believe that relationships involve being hurt or hurting others. The creation of a negative view about one's self can lead to a feeling of bondage. We learn to believe what people say to us, especially as children, and are held captive by those negative thoughts. We grow into the image of what we are taught to believe by those we love most and feel helpless to escape. DeMoss wrote, "feelings of worthlessness are the result of believing things we have heard from others, especially in childhood . . . The problem is that our view of ourselves and our sense of worth are often determined by the input and opinions of others" (2001, pp. 65-66). Moving away from the feeling of worthlessness to knowing who we are in Christ is the key element for helping women to escape addictive behaviors that tend to lead to additional self-destruction.

Prayer

Heavenly Father, as You have created the Heavens and the Earth You have created each of us to be an instrument that glorifies

You. Thank You for Your faithfulness to be available to us during both the good times and the bad. Allow us to grow in Your Word and understand that we are sinners and need to come to You for forgiveness and redemption. Take away the harmful habits and addictions that plague us and that build barriers between what You have created us to be and that which we have developed as harmful to ourselves and others. Remind us Lord that we belong to You and to no other and that we need You to guide us to full health and inner peace. In Your name we pray, Amen

Conclusion

Addictive behavior will be a significant part of the lives of some women you will encounter. The addictions can range from drug abuse, alcoholism, fear, depression, eating disorders, sexual abuse, and much more. "A man is a slave to whatever has mastered him" (2 Peter 2:19). Although women can come to God to find solace from the pain of addiction or any other life altering behaviors that hold them captive, more research and study is needed by any group leader to meet the needs of each individual problem. However, by using Scripture and prayer, much can be accomplished as a devoted servant of God to help struggling women find their purpose in God's plan for them. Being open and honest will help the women feel comfortable to share their own concerns. Avoiding judgment and a tendency to find solutions are not the job of the leader, rather be loving, supportive, and encouraging at all times. Be consistent with follow through by becoming a positive role model who will speak truth with love and respect. It is the leader's job to lift up God in all things and show the hurting that He is the answer to any problem.

CHAPTER 3

Facing A Sinful Nature:
Recognition

If we claim to be without sin, we deceive ourselves
and the truth is not in us. If we confess our sins, he
is faithful and just and will forgive us our sins and
purify us from all unrighteousness. 1 John 2:8-9

The first step for healing, regardless of the concern, is that
of recognizing the problem and addressing the realization
that the troubling issues are evident and real. Women
who live in crisis are no different. It is easy to avoid the issues and
put them aside or to blame others for their lot in life. Once the sin
is acknowledged then the healing may begin. Often the women
I work with find it difficult to take ownership in the sin and use
avoidance to address and accept the need to make significant
change. The Life Application Bible provides a good example of
how sin is viewed by God.

Christians commit sins, of course, but they ask God
to forgive them, and then they continue serving Him.
God has freed believers from their slavery to Satan,
and he keeps them safe from Satan's continued attacks.

The rest of the world does not have the Christian's freedom to obey God. Unless they come to Christ in faith, they have no choice but to obey Satan. There is no middle ground; people either belong to God and obey him, or they live under Satan's control. (NIV, 2005, p. 2127)

As most of us are aware, change is difficult and often painful. We are expected to move from our comfort zone into the unknown. There will be times when we find that the needed change is not what was expected and certainly not as easy to manage as we had hoped. Some women will move quickly into the realization that change is needed; others will fight the change and slowly move toward accepting the fact that they are the only people who can decide to face, or recognize, the issues and thus move toward a healthier outcome. As I worked on this book, I found a passage in the Life Application Study Bible from the Psalms that spoke volumes to me and is as follows:

Sometimes our burdens seem more than we can bear, and we wonder how we can go on. David stands at this bleak intersection of life's road and points toward the Lord, the great burden-bearer. God is able to lift us up because (1) his greatness is unfathomable (144:3); (2) he does mighty acts across many generations (145:4); (3) he is full of glorious splendor and majesty (145:5); (4) he does wonderful and awesome works (145: 5,6); (5) he is righteous (145:7); (6) he is gracious, compassionate, patient, and loving (145:8,9); (7) he rules over an everlasting kingdom (145:13); (8) he is our source of all our daily needs (145:15,16); (9) he is righteous and loving in all his dealings (145: 17); (10) he remains near to those who call on him (145:18); (11) he hears our cries and saves us (145:19, 20); If you are bending under a burden and feel that you are about to fall, turn to God for help. He is ready to lift you up and bear your burden. (NIV, 2005, p. 979)

Therefore, recognition that a problem exists and is keeping us separate from God's plan for us is the first step in understanding the need to make a change. The following Scriptures may be used to help reinforce the need to first recognize that there is a problem and then accept the fact that God is with us and willing to help us face our problems.

The following Scriptures provide biblical support for the principle of recognition of our sin:

- You who are trying to be justified by law have been alienated from Christ; you have fallen away from grace. But by faith we eagerly await through the Spirit the righteousness for which we hope. Galatians 5:5,6
- Oh, righteous God, who searches minds and hearts; bring to an end the violence of the wicked and make the righteous secure. Psalm 7:9
- Come to me, all you who are weary and burdened, and I will give you rest. Matthew 11: 28
- Be still and know that I am God. Psalm 46:10
- You were taught, with regard to you former way of life, to put off your old self, which is being corrupted by its deceitful desires, to be made new in the attitude of your minds; and to put on the new self, created to be like God in true righteousness and holiness. Ephesians 4:22-24

God's Presence

This then is how we know that we belong to the truth, and how set our hearts at rest in his presence whenever our hearts condemn us. For God is greater than our hearts, and he knows everything. 1 John 3:19-20

I often hear from the women I work with that they know God is *out there* but they just cannot feel His presence. Those who are living with self-destructive behaviors often are at a place in life where they need, or think they need, immediate help. They have made poor decisions that have led them down a path of self-deprivation leaving them with a feeling of despair and hopelessness; they call out to God when they are fighting personal demons or when they are completely consumed with fear, anger, or confusion. They often tell me that things are just too hard and they do not have the strength to move forward in a better light. Yes, trouble comes to us all. We make wrong decisions that hurt others and ourselves. I have often heard women say to me that they feel they have *crossed the line* and there is no *going back*. I have worked with several women who claim that their sin is so bad that God could not possibly forgive them. Although it can be a hard sell convincing some that even their sin is forgiven and forgotten, it can also be both rewarding and satisfying to know you have helped them begin to recognize the need to take ownership in the situation. It is important to help others realize that once they admit they have sinned and ask God to be a part of their lives and to provide forgiveness where they have failed, their lives can be completely turned over to Him. The first step is *recognizing* they need God in their lives and that they have sinned. Impress upon them that they cannot make it without His love and guidance and that love and guidance belongs to them just for the asking.

We have to be careful how we present God's love for others. Comfort (2010) reminds us that when we teach about sin, it is a fallacy to think that following God's way as all peace, love, and joy. He states:

> Many modern evangelistic appeals say, "Put on the Lord Jesus Christ. He'll give you love, joy, peace, fulfillment, and lasting happiness." The sinner responds, and in an experimental fashion puts on the Savior to see if the claims are true. And what does he get? Promised temptation, tribulation and persecution. (p. 71)

The author continues with reminding us that the promises of all problems being vanquished simply by professing a promise to follow Christ, can lead to short time commitment because the new believer will find the challenge only gets more difficult. Recognizing we are sinful by nature is the first step, but never can we claim that Satan will *back off* and leave us alone. Rather, Satan will step it up a notch and fight harder for us, leaving us to face possible ridicule, disillusionment, and anger that the promises of a happier existence were not kept.

What is Sin?

> . . . and everything that does not come from faith is sin. Romans 14:23b

We are no different from anyone else who struggles with the challenges life presents to us. However, those of us who follow God's plan will receive His promise of a life full of all that we need (2 Peter 1: 3). In Romans we find encouragement to take the difficulties as a means to develop personal strength based on the faith we have in Christ. "Therefore, since we have been justified through faith, we have peace with God through our Lord Jesus Christ, through whom we have gained access by faith into this grace in which we now stand. And we rejoice in the hope of the glory of God. Not only so, but we also rejoice in our sufferings, because we know that suffering produces perseverance; perseverance, character, and character hope" (Romans 5:1-4). Peter also writes, "For all have sinned and fall short of the glory of God" (Romans 3:23). Additionally, Peter writes, "Therefore, just as sin entered the world through one man, and death through sin, and in this way death came to all men, because all sinned" (Romans 5:12). This tells us that sin is universal and it applies to all of us.

As a member of the society in which you live, it is likely that sin is often recognized in an obvious frame of mind. We tend to recognize obvious sin, sin that is easily identified and perhaps labeled under the premise of what the law allows. Because we, as human beings live by what we see rather than by faith, it may be that the effects or result of our sin is not always recognized or understood. We forget, or maybe do not understand, that sin becomes the negative result of less noticeable actions that eventually do lead to a more destructive behavior. An example could be when a person begins drinking at parties. Drinking may be acceptable in your circle of friends and although you are willing to turn over your car keys to the designated driver you have still impaired yourself to be able to be attentively mindful of your altered actions. Eventually, you find that you are unable to meet your obligations without first masking the stress of the situation with alcohol. You convince yourself that you do not really need to drink but you accept it just to *take the edge off* of the situation. At first the alcohol gives you courage to face a dilemma but later you realize you cannot face the day without first having a drink.

A single drink leads to another until you find your relationships breaking down, you are in trouble with the law from time to time, and the self-destruction continues. Where is the sin? How does it affect your relationship with others? How does it affect your relationship with God? It is also necessary to understand that there are no particular levels of sin; Sin is sin. Sin does not have to be visible to those around you. Yes, it is easy to see when a murderer has sinned; the results are obvious. However, what about he or she who wishes someone to be hurt or even killed? What about hoping that your neighbor loses what they have because you do not want to live next to them any more? And what about that *little white lie*? Is any lie a little lie? According to the Life Application Bible (NIV, 2005), the definition of sin is "violation of conscience or of divine law; missing the mark; falling short of God's perfect standard" (p. 2364). Additionally, we learn that "everything that does not come from faith is sin" which means that going against a conviction will leave a person with a guilty or uneasy conscience. "When God shows us that something is wrong for us, we should avoid it" (p. 1906).

Discussion Points

Because we rely on God to be faithful as He promised, we look to Him to guide us in our daily walk. We realize sin is part of that walk although we strive to avoid sin and to become more Christ-like. We must admit (recognize) we are sinful by nature but that God never gives up on us as His own children. We are completely watched over by God as our Heavenly Father. We learn in the book of Romans that ". . . all sin deserves punishment. Instead of punishing us with the death we deserve however, Christ took our sins upon himself and took our punishment by dying on the cross"

(Life Application Study Bible, NIV, 2005, p. 1889). An area that leads us to commit sin may be in the form of idols we have come to acquire over time. Our human tendency to think selfishly can cause us to sin when the idols replace our devotion to God. We are taught that an idol can be anything that we elevate above trusting God (money, drugs, alcohol, prestige, etc.); putting trust in things that cannot save us from an eternal life with God. Does God punish us for serving the idols that consume our time and money? (Exodus 20:3). Use the following story from the Bible to guide your responses to the questions that follow regarding sin and punishment.

Read John 8: 1-11 (Jesus Forgives an Adulterous Woman)

"But Jesus went to the Mount of Olives. At dawn he appeared again in the temple courts, where all the people gathered around him, and he sat down to teach them. The teachers of the law and the Pharisees brought in a woman caught in adultery. They made her stand before the group and said to Jesus, 'Teacher, this woman was caught in the act of adultery. In the Law Moses commanded us to stone such women. Now what do you say?' they were using the question as a trap in order to have a basis for accusing him."

"But Jesus bent down and started to write on the ground with his finger. When they kept on questioning him, he straightened up and said to them, 'if any one of you is without sin, let him be the first to throw a stone at her.' Again he stooped down and wrote on the ground.

"At this, those who heard began to go away one at a time, the older ones first, until only Jesus was left, with the woman still standing there. Jesus straightened up and asked her, 'Woman, where are they? Has no one condemned you?'

"No one, sir," she said.

"Then neither do I condemn you." Jesus declared. "Go now and leave your life of sin."

a. What does this Scripture say to you about sin?

b. What does this scripture say to you about who sins and who does not?

c. What does this Scripture say to you about judging others?

d. When have you found yourself judging those who are different from yourself?

e. In what way would you like to be judged when you are caught in sin?

f. What does the Bible tell us about forgiveness in this passage from John?

g. What does it mean when the Bible tells us that Christ died for our sins?

h. We often hear the definitions of mercy and grace as follows:
   Grace: Receiving that which we *do not* deserve
   Mercy: Not receiving that which we *do* deserve

In the light of our discussion about sin, what do these definitions mean to you?

The Scripture is important because it illustrates that Jesus did not actually disobey the custom of stoning administered under the law when a person is caught in sin. However, by challenging those ready to cast judgment by stoning, he has illustrated compassion and understanding for the woman by asking each person to look at themselves in the light of sinning. Note that it is only God's role to sit in judgment of our sin; it is not our job to do so; Not for ourselves or for others.

Prayer

Dear Lord, thank You for being with us here and thank You for Your ever-present love for us, no matter what we have done to disappoint You. Help us to realize we all sin and that You are ready to help us recognize the sin so we can begin to make needed changes. We understand that it is not our place to judge others and we thank You for the grace and mercy that You offer to us each day. We praise You in all things. In Jesus' name pray, Amen.

God's Faithfulness

> Your kingdom is an everlasting kingdom, and your dominion endures through all generations. The Lord is faithful to all his promises and loving toward all he has made. Psalm 145:13

We often hear that we should be faithful to God and His Word by looking to Him and then trusting Him to help us remove ourselves from sin. But, what does it mean when we talk about God's faithfulness? How does this idea connect with what we believe to be true about faith? How does God's faithfulness relate to sin and how does His faithfulness relate to us as we honestly address our own sin? God's faithfulness is evident throughout the Bible. Such as, just a few notes regarding God's faithfulness in the book of Psalms includes a statement that God is faithful in all things (33:4); his faithfulness will not forsake (37:28); he sends us his faithfulness (57:3); His faithfulness endures (117:2) and; he is faithful to His promises (145:13).

The Life Application Bible (NIV, 2005) defines faithfulness as; firm in adherence; loyal; worthy of trust; devotion (p. 2326). Living in a secular world, we often make judgments based on what we can see and experience physically. This is being science-minded over spiritual-mindedness. Walking in faith is having trust in that which we cannot see. To fully trust in God we draw upon our ability to have faith in what is taught in the Bible. It is not always easy to have faith, we struggle with holding on to the unseen, but if we learn to walk in faith it will become easier to master. "The more we surrender our desire to walk by sight, the deeper our trust grows. We will begin to experience the freedom of living by faith" (Heald, 2000, p. 34).

It is common for people to think about how to develop a personal faith with a desire to be drawn closer to God through His son Jesus Christ. God's faith in us is more pronounced than we even realize. We know this because the Bible teaches us that He does not give up on us. He has faith in us to come closer to Him. However, this means making a deliberate choice. Following Christ does not come automatically but rather takes a concerted effort to learn and grow in understanding who He is and how we can connect with Him. People will follow Christ in the way in which it makes the most sense to them because we are all uniquely created. Ortberg writes, "Our individual uniqueness means we will all experience God's presence and learn to relate to him in different ways" (p. 120). Much of who we are is developed throughout our childhood and molded by many different people and different situations. But, we cannot use what the past has given to us as an excuse to refuse God in our lives. What happens to us in the past as children cannot be helped. We cannot change those events and we are not held accountable for them. However, we also cannot use that which was done to us as a crutch or excuse to be angry and unwilling to go to God for healing.

When reviewing God's Word, it is interesting to find that faith is prevalent within the very first book of the Bible, indicating God's early expectation of faith as necessary in relationship with Him. Through the story of Abraham and Sarah (Sarai) in Genesis

16, we learn that without faith we will face a series of problems. Take time to review the story and watch for evidence of God's desire to bless, the importance of waiting on God's timing, and His faithfulness to provide what He promised. You will find that God made a covenant with Abraham and because Abraham was faithful to God's plan, regardless of how impossible it seemed, he was blessed just as God promised. However, it took time for Abraham to follow God as closely as he should have. God had promised Abraham a son but still, as according to the customs of the time, sired a child with a servant girl when Sarah asked him to do so. Later, Sarah and the servant (Hagar) were at odds and Sarah became angry with Abraham for doing exactly what she asked him to do. Instead of having faith that God would provide as He promised, they all took the matter into their own hands instead of waiting on God. Later, God did provide Abraham and Sarah with a son as promised and Abraham's faith was strengthened once more.

Although we addressed God's faithfulness earlier, it is necessary to continue to work on this aspect of understanding God's purpose in our lives. Part of understanding faith, in what God tells us through the words in the Bible, is the development of trust in using Scripture as the most relevant source of understanding God's voice. Take time to read the following Scriptures and reflect upon how each relates to where you are in your journey. Consider the relationship found in the Scriptures between that of trusting God to be faithful and being true to your own faith. What do you find to represent God's covenant or commitment to do as He promised He would do for His people? What is your understanding of commitment and a covenant with God?

The following Scriptures provide biblical support for the principle of God's faithfulness:

- Know therefore that the Lord your God is God; he is the faithful God, keeping his covenant of love to a thousand generations of those who love him and keep his commands. Deuteronomy 7:9
- He is the Rock, his works are perfect, and all his ways are just. A faithful God who does no wrong, upright and just is He. Deuteronomy 32:4
- For the Word of the Lord is right and true; He is faithful in all He does. Psalm 33:4
- Your love, O Lord, reaches to the heavens, Your faithfulness to the skies. Psalm 36:5
- Your faithfulness continues through all generations; You established the earth, and it endures. Psalm 119:90
- Let us hold unswervingly to the hope we profess, for He who promised is faithful. Hebrews 10:23
- Jesus Christ is the same yesterday and today and forever. Hebrews 13:8

Discussion Points

The stories of Abraham and Sarah within the book of Genesis are valid and reliable for our own understanding of having faith in what God promises. One area we are not always good at is that of waiting for God to fulfill what He tells us He will do. Being impatient is what got Abraham in trouble in the first place, instead of realizing God had a plan for the timing of the promise as well as the promise itself. Think about your own life and how many times God has asked you to wait on Him, even when the situation seems urgent.

Use the following questions to guide you through self-reflection about faith.

a. In the story of Abraham and Sarah, which of the characters do you relate to the most? Why?

b. Reflecting upon what was presented from Genesis, how does the story of Abraham and Sarah relate to our time now on Earth?

c. Does God still make promises or covenants with His people?

d. How do we know when God has blessed us with what He has promised? What is our responsibility in receiving God's gifts?

e. How do we wait on the Lord to provide what he has promised to us as based on Scripture?

f. What is keeping you from having faith in God to fulfill His promises?

g. What have you experienced that shows you how faithful God's love is?

h. Where do you hope to be by this time next year? In five years? In ten years? How strong is your faith to believe you will reach these goals?

i. What steps do you need to take in order to move forward to a better more fulfilled life that illustrates your understanding of God's faithfulness?

Prayer

Heavenly Father, we come here today to seek Your presence in our lives. We thank You for Your promises and the undying love that You have for us. Help us to grow in our faithfulness and learn how to wait on You for your perfect timing. We ask for strength to follow You when we become weary or confused about what You have planned for us. We thank You for not giving up on us and being faithful to Your promises. Please keep our eyes on You in all things at all times. In Your son's name, Amen.

When Doubt Happens

Everything is possible for him who believes. Mark 9:23b

For I am convinced that neither death nor life, neither angels nor demons, neither the present nor the future, nor any powers, neither height nor depth, nor anything else in all creation, will be able to separate us from the love of God that is in Christ Jesus our Lord. Romans 8:38-39

Our belief in God and His son, Jesus Christ, comes from personal growth as we develop faith in what the Bible tells us. It is a growing process that lasts a lifetime and comes to be strengthened through daily prayer and obedience to the Word. God has given us the ability to have faith in Him, "For it is by grace you have been saved, through faith—and this not from yourselves, it is the gift of God" (Ephesians 2:8-9), but it is something that continues to grow stronger over time. This does not mean there will be no times of doubt. God allows us to ask for help with our disbelief or lack of faith when we feel alone and helpless in our doubt. We read about doubt in the story told through Mark, "immediately the boy's father exclaimed, I do believe; help me overcome my unbelief!" (9:24).

As we think about how doubt intertwines with our faith, we should also think about the part we play and how it relates to what happens to us. It is easy to blame someone else when life becomes difficult and does not turn out as we planned. In many cases, we blame God for *allowing* trouble to interfere with our happiness and prosperity. Instead, look first within and determine what you may have done to cause the difficulties you are facing. Have you committed to something that would be considered sinful in

God's eyes? Are your decisions pleasing to God? God gives us free will to be human and make mistakes; He also expects us to be obedient, as He has commanded all humankind to do in His name. If we choose to ignore what God expects, then we choose to face the consequences from sinful actions. God has warned us throughout the Bible that disobedience most definitely does have consequences. A few such warnings are found in Genesis 2:17, "but you must not eat from the tree of the knowledge of good and evil, for when you eat of it you will surely die"; Proverbs 13:15, "Good understanding wins favor, but the way of the unfaithful is hard"; Ezekiel 18:13, "He lends at usury and takes excessive interest. Will such a man live? He will not! Because he has done all these detestable things, he will surely be put to death and his blood will be on his own head"; Romans 2:9, "There will be trouble and distress for every human being who does evil: first for the Jew, then for the Gentile." As God shows us through these examples, we have free will to do what we please. But, we have also been warned that our choices can lead to destruction. Thankfully, God does not give up on us and is willing to help us find the path back to Him through His mercy and grace.

When doubt consumes us we fall further from God's will for us. We discussed earlier that God is faithful and will not give up, but we, too, must not give up. First we cannot give up on God's promises and secondly we cannot give up on ourselves. I am not suggesting that life will become easy at every turn. After all, Satan is playing a significant part in our lives as well. If you are at a place in your life where you are held emotionally or physically captive by the poor choices you have made, then Satan has held you in his power for a long time. He does not give up easily and is ready for a fight. In Ephesians 6: 11-12 we read, "put on the full armor of God so that you can take your stand against the devil's schemes. For our struggle is not against flesh and blood, but against the rulers, against the authorities, against the powers of this dark world and against the spiritual forces of evil in the heavenly realms." Paul is warning us that evil is around us and will always be part of the physical and spiritual world as long as we allow Satan to continue to be a part of our lives. It is a choice of whether you wish to follow Christ or continue to be a slave belonging to Satan. Therefore, when doubt consumes us we can assume Satan is trying to interfere with our connection to God and will do all he can to keep us under his control.

Discussion Points

One story about doubt found in the Bible is that of the demon possessed boy who is brought to Jesus for healing. Read the three versions of the story of Jesus healing the demon-possessed boy as found in Mark 9:14-29, Matthew 17:14-21, and Luke 9:37-43.

a. What point does Jesus make about the faith of His disciples?

b. How does this story relate to our tendency to doubt?

c. When do you most likely find yourself doubting?

d. What does it take for your doubt to be restored?

e. What will you do the next time you begin to doubt that God is the master of your life?

Prayer

Lord, You already know everything we have done in our lives, regardless of how good or bad the decisions have been. You have never left our side and yet sometimes we still doubt You are with us. When things are hard and fear consumes us, we know our human emotions can get in the way. Help us, Lord, with our doubts and disbelief. We need You with us every day in every situation. Please remind us to turn to You before a decision is made. Help us know we do not have to react, but can take time to think and pray about things before decisions are made. Help us to remove Satan from our lives by trusting in You and You alone. We ask all of this in Your son's name, Amen.

Speaking to God Through Prayer

> And pray in the Spirit on all occasions with all kinds of prayers and requests. Ephesians 6:18a.

I have often heard people say that God speaks to us through our prayers. He will answer when we call upon Him in faith. The point is, though, He may not answer your prayer in the way you want Him to. He may answer with a blessed *yes,* or possibly with a resounding *no* because He knows what is best for you, more than you could ever imagine, because only He knows the future. Finally, He could even answer with something as simple as *not now* or *wait, I have something even better for you.* In some ways the *not now* answer is more difficult to manage than to just know one way or the other what God wants us to do. The point is that we must use faith to call upon God to be our solution to any problem or request that we have. With a strong faith comes an internal assurance that God is in control and will do what is best in any situation.

It is not uncommon for some individuals to struggle with prayer. They feel uncomfortable humbling themselves before God. Some have experienced a lifetime of church friends or family members who seem to have all the right words when they pray aloud. Many of us have had that special grandparent who could call upon the Lord in a way that caused us to believe that there was no way God would not answer and answer quick. I grew up thinking if I just could say the right words then God would pay closer attention. Thank goodness I have learned that God listens to our heart and not just to our words. Unfortunately, many of us have gotten into a bad habit of going about our own business and then retrospectively asking God to bless our activities rather than asking God to show us the way *before* we act (Cymbala, 2003).

It can become a challenge and concern for someone not comfortable praying aloud especially when they feel they do not have the words that are required to make a prayer really work. What a blessing when someone comes to realize that prayer is not about the words, it is about the feeling behind the thoughts that are behind the prayer. When working with my ladies I share with them the ongoing conversation I have with Jesus in my daily life. It is not uncommon for me to say *thank you, Jesus,* out loud in my car when a good parking spot magically appears just when I need it. I have sighed a breath of relief while thanking Jesus for keeping the jar of spaghetti sauce balanced carefully on the grocery store shelf as I bumped up against it. And I always say thank you for safety when driving through city traffic. I have a very dear Aunt who, from the time her sons were born, would pray for them every time she sat behind the wheel of her car. It is a life long habit she developed to remind her to pray each day for her family. The point here is that we should always be in an attitude of prayer throughout every day and develop a thankful spirit in all things, regardless of how trivial they may seem at the time. Be in full conversation with Jesus all day long; Make Him a part of your daily thoughts and actions. The Life Application Bible supports this premise when they shared:

> How can anyone pray on all occasions? One way is to make quick, brief prayers your habitual response to every situation you meet throughout the day. Another way is to order your life around God's desires and teachings so that your very life becomes a prayer. You don't have to isolate yourself from other people and from daily work in order to pray constantly. You can make a prayer your life and your life a prayer while living in a world that needs God's powerful influence. (2005, NIV, p. 1990)

Another point I would like to make about prayer involves being humble enough to ask others to pray for you. It is not easy to admit when we fail. To admit we have failed God is even more difficult and can be a scary thing for most people to do. I have always found it easy to request prayer for a friend or family member who is suffering with illness or other personal struggles, but asking for myself was not as easy. Somehow it felt selfish on my part. Praying for each other is necessary as part of God's family, but we should also be willing to ask others to pray for us. There are times in our lives when we become spiritually fatigued and are so weighed down by the troubles of our lives that we cannot find the strength to reach out to God, as we should. This is the time we call upon those around us to pray on our behalf. I do this often for the women I work with to show them that prayer is a life line between us and God's kingdom and that we can pray for each other, especially when we just cannot pray for ourselves. It is not uncommon for me to ask someone if I may pray for him or her, after they have shared a fear or concern with me. The point is to reach out and pray for those who may not be able to do it for themselves regardless of the reason.

Discussion Points

Read each of the following Scriptures and then reflect on what the words say to you personally. Think of a situation when you have used each example of prayer as used in the following Scriptures.

> a. Matthew 6:7-And when you pray, do not keep on babbling like pagans, for they think they will be heard because of their many words.
>
> • Have you experienced this kind of prayer from others or in your own prayer life? What does the Scripture say to you?

b. II Chronicles 7:14-If my people, who are called by my name, will humble themselves and pray and seek my face and turn from their wicked ways, then will I hear from heaven and will forgive their sin and will heal their land.

- What is God saying in this verse? What does it mean to humble yourself and seek His face? How do we do this in our daily lives?

c. Romans 8:26-In the same way, the Spirit helps us in our weakness. We do not know what we ought to pray for, but the Spirit himself intercedes for us with groans that words cannot express.

- What is the *Spirit* in this verse? Explain what the entire verse means to you regarding your own prayer life.

d. I Thessalonians 5:17-18-Pray continually; give thanks in all circumstances, for this is God's will for you in Christ Jesus.

- How do you interpret what is meant by *pray continually*? What does it mean to give thanks in all circumstances? Have you ever been faced with trying to be thankful when life is difficult?

e. Philippians 4:6-Do not be anxious about anything, but in everything, by prayer and petition, with thanksgiving, present your request to God. And the peace of God, which transcends all understanding, will guard your hearts and your minds in Christ Jesus.

- How are we to pray, according to this Scripture? What part of this verse speaks loudest to you in its meaning about prayer?

Take time to speak to God privately and ask that He show you where and what He wants you to do next. Use some quiet time to do this and bow your head and close your eyes.

Leader Notes: Because this activity may be difficult for some, I model the activity by doing the same and after a few minutes I will say *amen* to indicate the end of the group prayer. The leader should also model the next activity. Ask each person to choose one word that they would like to speak aloud as if Jesus were visibly present at this moment. I emphasize that Jesus is already with us even though we cannot see Him in human form. I then illustrate by stating one word aloud and then ask each person to speak one word as well. After each word is spoken I will say a prayer for the group asking God to bless all of us and to help us know that He understands why each of us chose the word that we did.

Prayer

Dear God, we thank You for the opportunity to speak to You through our prayers and we thank You for always knowing just what we mean when we cannot verbalize our thoughts. Help us to remember that Your timing is always perfect timing and that You will answer our prayers even though it may not always be in the way we expect. We ask for blessing on each of us in all areas of our lives so that we are positive examples to others. Help us to make our daily activities a prayer to You and to feel free to speak to You on all occasions through the blessing of prayer. Thank You for being with us this day as we learn more about how to pray and follow You as true believers with faithful hearts. In Christ's name, Amen.

When and How Does God Speak?

> For the sake of your Word and according to your will,
> you have done this great thing and made it known to
> your servant. 2 Samuel 8:21

So, we talk to God through our prayers but how does He talk to us? As mentioned earlier, God answers us in one of three ways; yes, no, or not now. But, how do we know when He is providing an answer? Although we would love to be like Abraham or Moses and hear God's voice telling us just what we are supposed to do, we must rely on God's direction through Jesus and learn to use prayer and faith to hear His direction for us. The Scripture above illustrates how God answers prayer through our circumstances and how God keeps His promises. God still answers prayer through a variety of means. Sometimes is it a message you needed to hear from a family member, a change in plans that you did not orchestrate, or a surprise blessing that you never expected. Consider the possibility of God speaking to you in the following ways:

- You develop a passion for doing something that keeps surfacing in your thoughts.
- Someone points out a talent they feel you have even though you never considered it before.
- Doors begin to open that lead to the financial support you need to go to school to study something of which you felt a strong interest.
- You receive a note in the mail from someone you admire who gives you a word of wisdom that helps you make a decision.
- Something unexpected occurs that appears to be more than just a coincidence.
- The pastor preaches on a topic that has been concerning you personally.
- You receive an unexpected gift in the mail or in person.
- You have a dream that seems to be guiding you in a particular direction.
- Someone offers friendship at a time you need it most.

Although these are only a few ideas, we have all seen events that have happened either in our own lives or in that of others we have known. The following experiences are examples of how God answers prayer in unusual ways.

- As a teacher, in 1986, it became financially evident that I needed to go back to school to earn a masters degree in order to earn a higher wage on the teacher's pay scale. I wasn't sure what area of interest to choose and was praying about that very thing in my classroom after school, when in walked my school principal. I had not told him I was planning on earning a masters degree but he asked me if I had ever considered going back to school to become a school administrator. I laughed out loud and said emphatically that I had absolutely no desire to be a principal. He just nodded, smiled, and said to think about it because he felt I would be a very good administrator. He also mentioned that a master's degree in administration would open doors for me in the future and would look very good on a resume. There was my answer, although completely unexpected. I thought a master's degree in reading or curriculum was the direction to go, but now I had a new idea. I admired my principal greatly and was honored that he thought I would be a good principal.

Results:
- I was chosen as one of 25 honored students to become a cadre member in a specially designed masters degree program.
- I finished in 15 months, instead of the usual 24 months.
- The assistant principal in my school resigned one month before I graduated
- The very man who suggested I consider becoming an administrator hired me as the new assistant principal.
- I received a $20,000 pay raise in the first year.

Conclusion: God gave me more than I asked for and he sent someone I admired to plant the seed for changing my life. All I asked for was direction, as to which degree program I should apply for, but God gave me a greater opportunity and my pay raise was more than I ever dreamed possible. I have never regretted the decision or the blessing God gave to me. Much of what happened in my career as an administrator helped to develop a heart for working with hurting people. God had a long-term plan for me that I was not able to see at the time, but now it is very evident what His plans were and I am thankful to have been blessed in this way.

- In 1999, I discovered I needed a medical procedure to help with a bladder problem. I had been putting it off because it really was not a big deal, or so I thought, and I certainly did not like the idea of surgery. I prayed about it and asked God to show me if He really thought this procedure was necessary. I called my doctor and asked for a consult. At that time he said the decision was up to me because it really was not a major problem and I could probably go for years and not need anything done. That evening I was online in an instant message format with my closest friend and told her about my difficult decision. She said her colleague had put off seeing a specialist and ended up dying of colon cancer. Had she gone to the doctor earlier they may have been able to save her through a preventative surgery. Oh, my, that got my attention! I felt God was showing me it would be a good idea to at least check it out with the specialist. I made my appointment and faced the discomfort of the tests.

Results:
- The test indicated I had bigger issues than I ever dreamed. I had inherited a birth defect that lead to major surgery and a long recovery. The problem had already begun to damage my kidney.
- The birth defect was so prevalent in females within families that I was able to warn all female cousins as well as my own sister so that they may also avoid a serious problem later in life.

- By having the surgery when I did, I saved a kidney. Had I put it off much longer I could have lost the kidney and faced a much more serious health risk.

Conclusion: God protected me by pushing me to see a specialist even though my regular doctor said there was no hurry. By praying about the decision, God showed me what needed to be done through the words of a dear friend. I discovered the importance of relying on Him and not just my own feelings of wanting to put things off.

- In 2009, the economy had taken a hard hit and the housing market was in bad shape. My husband and I had just bought a small home and had it completely remodeled. My husband had been retired for a year and the idea of living in a smaller home was very appealing so we were looking forward to making the move. When it became evident that our large house was not going to sell, we were not sure what to do next. We had no idea of how we could pay for two homes when he was now unemployed and not old enough for social security. We had wanted to downsize and rid ourselves of the high cost of our large home in a retirement community. All we knew to do was to pray about it and ask God to show us the way. One day my husband had a strong feeling that he needed to go see an old friend that he had not seen in some time (He calls this a God thing). When he met this friend he was told that the owner of a company, similar to what my husband had done his entire career, was looking for him. Being curious, my husband called this man to see what he needed. What a blessing! The owner of the company was looking for someone like my husband to work for him.

Results:

- My husband met with the company's owner the next day.
- He was hired to begin a great job two days later.
- The job is the best job he has ever had, he has the nicest boss he has ever worked for, and he is making more money than he has ever made at any other job.

Conclusion: We have no doubt that by deciding to turn our concerns over to God and let Him work out the details; our situation was taken care of. My husband was blessed with more than he dreamed. We could have walked away from one of the homes, as many people were doing at that time, but we felt God would show us what to do with the problem, and His answer was bigger and better than we ever anticipated. God is so good!

The three examples shared are only a few of what could be discussed. But the point is that God is faithful in answering our prayers when we trust Him. God uses whatever and whomever He wishes to provide the answers we need. It is our job to pay attention and to be open to His leading. Some of the most delightful experiences come from an answered prayer that is answered in a way we never thought of on our own. Ortberg wrote about the power of prayer through trusting that God will always be there to hear us. The author explains that prayer that is honest, passionate, and open, will help to build spiritual health. "God will create the kind of condition in our heart that will make resting in his presence possible again, and God will come. But he may come in unexpected ways" (2005, p. 161). God blesses us abundantly when we are faithful to His purpose. And sometimes that blessing is in human form.

<u>Leader Notes:</u> An area that women in crisis often struggle with is in the knowing of what or how to pray. They understand they are in crisis, they realize they have made poor, and at times dangerous, decisions, they accept that they have chosen a life of sin. But, how do they pull themselves out of the depths of despair, fear, and complete mental exhaustion? How can prayer possibly be the answer even when it seems simple enough, although the words may not seem readily available? Where do they begin, really? What do they do first and how do they do it? I use the following steps to lead my women to learn to rely on prayer as a first step to redemption:

1. Admit you are sinning against God's plan through the choices you have made.
2. Ask God to forgive you for hurting yourself and others.
3. Ask God to help you with your disbelief or your doubt.
4. Thank Him for the answers you need, even if you are not sure what they are.

Discussion Points

Because we know that God speaks to us through others as well as through our circumstances, it is imperative that we learn to trust Him to take care of us as He promises. Faith comes from within and is evident in our actions. Discuss the following questions and share how each of them touches your own life.

a. In what ways have you experienced God speaking to you?

b. What do you find most difficult about the concept of prayer?

c. With whom in your life do you feel comfortable to discuss questions about God or to ask to pray for you?

d. If you could choose one word to describe prayer, what would it be? Why did you choose this word?

e. How does it feel to know that God is a part of all things and knows all that we do?

f. Privately think of an area in your life where you feel a need to make change in order to draw closer to God.

Prayer

Thank You Lord, for Your faithfulness, for always showing us that You love us. Help us to recognize the people You place in our lives to walk with us as we learn to understand Your plan. Help us to learn to pray and receive Your blessings with thankful hearts.

Forgive us when we fail to do what You are calling us to do. We want to please You and grow in the understanding of Your will as we learn more about You and the love You have for us. Strengthen our trust so that we are trustworthy and loving models to other people. In Your son's name we pray, Amen.

God Speaks Hope to Our Hearts

There is surely a future hope for you, and your hope will not be cut off. Proverbs 23:18

"For I know the plans I have for you," declares the Lord, "plans to prosper you and not to harm you, plans to give you hope and a future." Jeremiah 29:11

May the God of hope fill you with all joy and peace as you trust in him, so that you may overflow with hope by the power of the Holy Spirit. Romans 15:13

When we reach a place in our lives where we feel we cannot go another step and that all possible change or opportunity is lost, we have two choices; give in and give up or place our hope in the arms of Jesus. Of course I would vote for using hope to push us forward rather than to give up and live in despair and crisis. However, I am not saying gathering up the strength to rely on hope is an easy thing when you are living in your darkest moments, in pain, or feel completely alone. The good news is, however, hope is never out of reach. All we have to do is ask God to help us find it when we feel most lost; Ask, trust, wait, receive. Pastor Swindoll once wrote, "Hope is a wonderful gift from God, a source of strength and courage in the face of life's harshest trials" (2002, p. 142). The trials he speaks of are not limited to what happens to us against our will, but also includes the messes we are in due to our own choices. Sometimes it feels like we cannot go one step forward because there is no going back and fixing what went wrong. The beauty in what Pastor Swindoll claims is that relying on God to give us hope is a free gift God offers all of us. We do not have to earn it; He is offering it for free! In the Swindoll book, The Strength of Character, the author lists several areas in life when hope will help us take the first step toward change:

- When we are trapped in a tunnel of misery, hope points to the light at the end.
- When we are discouraged, hope lifts our spirits.
- When we have lost our way and confusion blurs the destination, hope dulls the edge of panic.
- When we fear the worst, hope brings reminders that God is still in control.
- When we must endure the consequences of bad decisions, hope fuels our recovery.
- When we are forced to sit back and wait, hope gives us the patience to trust.
- When we feel rejected and abandoned, hope reminds us we're not alone . . . we'll make it. (2002, pp. 142-143)

Each of us have had times in our lives when we needed to have hope in order for us to take the necessary steps to correct a wrong, make a decision, or face a difficult situation. Learning to hold on to the hope that God provides is a good first step toward facing the challenges we all experience from time to time. It does not mean that we will not have to wait to have our prayers answered, with patience and perseverance, but hope does provide the strength we need to move forward with intention and purpose.

I would like to share some information from the book Lies Women Believe: And the Truth That Sets Them Free, by DeMoss (2001). This book explains several areas in the lives of women where self-esteem and self-worth are addressed, which often leads to a feeling of hopelessness. Pointing out how women tend to believe the lies we are told about ourselves can be determined as a message from Satan. After all, he is victorious when we fail or turn away from God. This is where the principle of hope comes in to play. Without having hope in Christ, we would fall into the trap of listening to the enemy instead of listening to the one who created us as beautiful relational beings. DeMoss suggests that what we believe directly influences our behavior and therefore that behavior will indicate what we believe. "We listen to the lie; we dwell on it until we believe it; finally, we act on it" (p. 39). From the lie grows self-destruction and despair, which in turn can lead to sinful actions. "A man is a slave to whatever has mastered him" (II Peter 2:19b). However, as God's children, we always have a hope in Him because we are lovely in His eyes and created in His image. He wants only the best for us and asks that we do not give up hope in Him as the answer we need to be fully blessed. "May our Lord Jesus Christ himself and God our Father, who loved us and by his grace gave us eternal encouragement and good hope, encourage your hearts and strengthen you in every good deed and word" (2 Thessalonians 2:16-17).

Discussion Points

Having hope is something all of us need to work on as we face challenges that lead to a feeling of despair or a desire to give up. Knowing God is the answer, no matter what, can test the faith of all of us as children of God. It is easy to claim hope when things are going well, but when life becomes difficult we tend to run away from the issues rather than running toward God. The following questions will help you think about your level of hope in God's promises that He is the answer to whatever you are questioning.

a. When do you feel most hopeless about your situation?

b. What can you do the next time you become afraid and need to think about finding hope?

c. List three things you hope will happen in the next few weeks:
   1.

   2.

   3.

d. What is the difference between hoping for something and relying on our God of hope?

e. Write a personal definition of hope as we have discussed it together.

<u>Leader Notes:</u> Women who are held captive by addictive behaviors or harmful choices are less likely to remain in the state of self-destruction if they continue to find hope in what God has promised. It is unrealistic to consider this effort to be a *quick fix*, but the worth behind the effort is far reaching as we seek recovery and redemption, found only when we turn to God for the answers we need. Seeking freedom is not about doing just what we want to do but rather following God's plan rather than "our own sinful desires and become enslaved to what our bodies want" (Life Application Bible, NIV, 2005, p. 2115). Become aware that the women who are struggling with addiction may fall back from time to time. It is a hard road to escape the control of that which controls our mind and body, especially when we are new to seeking God's voice. Remember, although God is all-powerful and able to help heal the afflicted, Satan is also part of that which is negative in the lives of these women. He has had control of them for a long time and will not easily give them up. Patience and perseverance remains instrumental in helping a women walk away from Satan's control. Hope is a concept of which women held in bondage may not fully understand or have experienced. The leader may be the source of hope at this point in the program and it is perfectly fine to be that hope for the woman who is learning to turn to God. Lead by example and share the many times you have relied on hope in Christ to pull you through tough times.

Prayer

Our Heavenly Father we ask for Your guidance as we learn to watch for the signs of Your presence through the events and people in our lives. Help us to recognize our sin and to hear Your voice so that it becomes easier to draw closer to You. Thank You for being the answer to all of our difficulties and for loving us no matter what we have done to disappoint You. Search our hearts, Lord, and show us the path to Your kingdom. Remind us to keep You in our thoughts each day as part of our prayer life and to be thankful in all things. We rely on our hope in You and will continue to trust You as we are called into obedience. In Jesus' name, Amen.

Conclusion

The first step for hearing God's voice is to first *recognize* the fact that we need God in our lives. To recognize this need may come from finding ourselves unable to face the day with any form of hope or joy in our hearts. We often hear about those who *have hit their lowest point* or who *have hit bottom*. Regardless of what you call it, recognizing the fact that you can no longer do it on your own is the first step to reaching out to God and asking Him to walk with you. Build on your faith with full understanding that Satan is also fighting for his control over you and can cause havoc with your ability to develop a strong conviction that God is with you no matter what. Make an effort to pray in faithfulness and expect God to answer in His time. Think about those around you who may be a positive influence in your search for God's voice. Our sin is never hidden from God. He knows everything we have done and loves us any way. What a great promise! God loves us and wants only the best for us as we continue to have hope in Him. He blesses us in many ways, all of which are designed to bring a deeper understanding of His purpose for us. It is our job to be faithful, obedient to His Word, and continue to work toward developing an attitude of acceptance for what He wants to do in our lives.

CHAPTER 4

Calling Out to God:
Repent

The Lord is not slow in keeping his promise, as some understand slowness. He is patient with you, not wanting anyone to perish, but everyone to come to repentance. 2 Peter 3:9

"I tell you that in the same way there will be more rejoicing in heaven over one sinner who repents than over ninety-nine righteous persons who do not need to repent." Luke 15:7

Therefore, get rid of all moral filth and the evil that is so prevalent and humbly accept the word planted in you, which can save you. James 1:21

One definition for repentance comes from the NIV Application Study Bible (2005). The definition reads as "to experience sorrow for and seek to change wrong behavior" (p. 2359). When we read Scripture describing repentance we often focus on the idea of forgiveness. By all means, forgiveness is definitely an important element of repentance however we also often leave out the next most important element; NEVER DO IT AGAIN. One of my favorite ideas about making change in our behavior is with the idea of making a moral u-turn: 180 degrees moving away from the sin and toward repentance. The Life Application Bible (NIV, 2005) explains that to fully repent before God requires two distinct steps; turning away from sins and turning toward God (p. 1668). This means:

> The first step in turning to God is to admit your sin.
> Then God will receive you and help you live the way
> he wants. Remember that only God can get rid of sin.
> He doesn't expect us to clean up our lives before we
> come to him. (p. 1530)

Repentance through God's grace is a free gift and something easily obtained if we truly follow God's guidance. However, because we seek forgiveness for our sins, it is necessary to first repent, or rather own up to, our sins. Then ask God for forgiveness and renewal. We will discuss forgiveness more thoroughly in Chapter 5.

David asked God to forgive him for the sins he had committed but prior to being forgiven, David knew he had to speak honestly to God and admit his sinful ways. In 1 Chronicles 21:8 we learn that David took on the responsibility for his sin and spoke it aloud when he said "I have sinned greatly, because I have done this thing: but now, I pray, take away the iniquity of Your servant, for I have done very foolishly." David is admitting that he had done wrong in the eyes of his Lord and that he would need to speak it to God and take ownership of his sins before he could then humbly ask for forgiveness. Ownership is part of repenting. You need to own the sin, after all you did it, no one made you do it, you chose to sin or you would not have done it in the first place. Owning your sin can be uncomfortable and messy at times. It means having to admit something terrible; after all there is no such thing as a good sin. Instead of saying, "I made a mistake," speak boldly that you committed a sin and you realize it was something that goes against God's plan for you and for others.

The following Scriptures provide biblical support for the principle of repentance:

- In repentance and rest is your salvation, in quietness and trust is your strength. Isaiah 30:15a
- If you repent, I will restore you that you may serve me. Jeremiah 15:19
- Therefore, O house of Israel, I will judge you, each one according to his ways, declares the Sovereign Lord. Repent! Turn away from all your offenses; then sin will not be your downfall. Ezekiel 18:30
- . . . and saying, Repent, for the kingdom of heaven is near. Matthew 3:2
- And so John came, baptizing in the desert region and preaching a baptism of repentance for the forgiveness of sins. Mark 1:4
- I have not come to call the righteous, but sinners to repentance. Luke 5:32
- In the past God overlooked such ignorance, but now he commands all people everywhere to repent. Acts 17:30
- Or do you show contempt for the riches of his kindness, tolerance and patience, not realizing that God's kindness leads you toward repentance? Romans 2:4
- Godly sorrow brings repentance that leads to salvation and leaves no regret, but worldly sorrow brings death. 2 Corinthians 7:10

- The Lord is not slow in keeping his promise, as some understand slowness. He is patient with you, not wanting anyone to perish, but everyone to come to repentance. 2 Peter 3:9

What is Repentance?

Therefore, O house of Israel, I will judge you, each one according to his ways, declares the Sovereign Lord. Repent! Turn away from all your offenses; then sin will not be your downfall. Ezekiel 19:30

The Life Application Study Bible (2005) describes repentance as; "to experience sorrow for and seek to change wrong behavior" (p. 2359). Repentance can be thought of as a cleansing of the soul, a means to recognize the sin, or wrongdoing, and to remove it from practice by admitting the fault and claiming a change, never to repeat the transgression. Dr. David Jeremiah talks about how David came to God to repent and requested to be "cleansed of his moral degradation" (2001, p. 81). Dr. Jeremiah discussed how David felt unclean and remorseful in his petition to God for his forgiveness. Wash me thoroughly from my iniquity, and cleanse me from my sin (Psalm 51:2). So, we can assume that repentance is more than asking to be forgiven. It is a heartfelt urgency to have the sin removed and not repeated. Until we fully repent of the sin, forgiveness cannot occur.

True repentance is revealed by changed actions—to be sorry with a change of heart. When our hearts are changed, our actions will follow accordingly. To repent will require commitment to what God is asking us to do. He wants us to be committed to His purpose and His plan, which means to praise Him daily. This does not mean you are called to a life of comfort, but a life of full attention and energy placed on following Jesus. Submitting yourself to become God's disciple/follower becomes a mutual commitment between you and God. From this we can see that to repent fully means saying yes to God, but saying yes also means you may not always experience days of carefree abandon. Terkeurst (2007) wrote:

> Being a woman who says yes to God means making the choice to trust Him even when you can't understand why He requires some of the things He does. It also means that once you've said yes to God, you refuse to turn back, even when things get hard. (p. 16)

Look into yourself and decide if you are strong enough to give all of yourself to God. This means to trust in Him to show you what to do after you have made a commitment to follow Him. Believe that He has all of the details worked out for you and He is ready to bring you to Him offering all that life has to offer through obedience and purpose to His will. Can you give up your own will in order to follow His will? Mayes wrote the following to encourage us to stay faithful to our obedience:

> Keep your guard up. When you find yourself thinking that your behavior doesn't matter, recognize that it does. When obedience seems to make no difference, refuse to believe it. Your behavior matters whether you see the outcome of it or not. (1995, p. 140)

Yes, there will be times when it all seems very difficult and maybe even impossible. Fall to your knees, humble yourself before Him, and earnestly pray for His guidance in all things. Then release the worry and frustration. He will take it for you and carry the load. The bottom line is that if you are repenting then you are giving up that which holds you captive. You are ready to remove yourself from your old ways and begin a new life through God's son, Jesus Christ. Even David threw himself on the mercy of the Lord. "When he realized his sin, he took full responsibility, admitted he was wrong, and asked God to forgive him" (Life Application Bible, NIV, 2005, p. 633).

Leader Notes: As you work with women who wish to make major change in their lives by repenting of their sins and finding solace in that decision, you may find that the women fall back from time to time. However, as I have said before, having patience is the key. Big changes are not easily mastered and often do not happen with the first attempt. Recognize that Satan does not give up easily either and has every intention of holding on to the captive by using temptation and coercion to ensure the addiction or harmful decision-making continues.

Discussion Points

Repentance is difficult but necessary if we are to expect God's forgiveness for our sin. It is about the admission of guilt for what we have done that has caused hurt or damage to others or to us. To repent is to make it known to God that you realize and own up to the damages you have caused. It opens the door to forgiveness and healing. Omartian (2003) wrote, "when sin is left unconfessed, a wall goes up between you and God. Even though the sin may have stopped, it will still weigh you down" (p. 18). Take time to review the list below and circle the areas where you feel you have sinned in the past or areas whereby you are presently struggling.

- Anger with my parent(s)
- Negative thoughts about my boss/teacher
- Criticism of others
- Use of hurtful language
- Inappropriate use of God's name
- Physically hurting another
- Lusting
- Prideful thoughts
- Lying to others
- Shoplifting/theft
- Misuse of alcohol or drugs
- Self indulgence at the expense of others
- Not taking ownership for hurting another
- Rebelling against authority

Now think about anything else that may be causing you emotional or physical discomfort from unrepented sin. Silently say this prayer:

> Dear God in heaven, I know I have failed You in many ways during my lifetime. I am bringing the sins of the past and present to You and lay them at the foot of the cross. Help me to remove the sin from my life and to take ownership in areas where I need to make restitution to others. I confess my failures, Lord, and I ask that You forgive me for all of my indiscretions that have caused me to be separated from You. I know it takes time to heal from the brokenness I have experienced

but I want You to help me walk through the dark and
into the light. In Jesus' name I pray, Amen

Think about the following and choose steps that will help you
continue your journey to forgiveness. Which of the choices do
you feel would work best for you?

- Ask a trusted friend to listen to your confession of sins
  from the past and present.
- Seek out an older Godly woman to serve as a mentor for
  you.
- Join a Bible study for women that address healthy life
  styles.
- Ask forgiveness from someone you have hurt.
- Begin a daily devotional or Bible study at home.
- Begin a personal journal of reflection and prayer.
- Join a support group to address your addiction.
- Commit to daily prayer and meditation.
- What other ideas do you have?

Prayer

Our Heavenly Father, thank You for never giving up on us. Thank
You for being with us in the hard times as well as the times of
joy. Help us to find the strength and understanding it takes to
fully repent from those things we do that are not pleasing to You.
Help us to identify what it is that keeps us from being in complete
relationship with You. Show us the way, Lord, and help us to trust
You with the answers we seek. We know You have all of the details
worked out so show us how to turn away from the old self and
begin a new life in You. In Your son's name we pray, Amen.

Repentance with Forgiveness

> God exalted him to his own right hand as Prince and
> Savior that he might give repentance and forgiveness
> of sins to Israel. Acts 5:31

To continue with the idea of repentance let's think about how forgiveness aligns with a repentant heart. It is fairly easy to recognize when we need to ask for forgiveness and we can easily identify with others when they lay down their sins at the foot of the cross and ask God to forgive them for the sins they bring forth. However, Anton (2005) tells us "we cheapen grace when we reduce the gospel to forgiveness of sins only. And we discredit the message of God when we neglect the repentance of sins" (p. 17). We tend to want to do it all ourselves by claiming we can change without any help; that all we need to know is that God has forgiven the sin. This way of thinking will need to be adjusted if we desire God's presence in our lives. I especially liked what Anton said about making a shift in our thinking from self-centered to God-centered when he wrote:

> In order to shift to a paradigm of truth—I must admit
> to being sinful (not so hard), to being selfish (harder),
> and to being wrong (really, really hard). In the end,
> the ultimate paradigm shift places Jesus on the throne
> at the center of my life whereby I proclaim, 'Jesus—
> not self—is Lord!' (p. 53)

To admit and take ownership of our faults, especially those that cause damage to self or others, are difficult and at times seems quite impossible. We can fall into the trap of assuming all hope is gone; that we do not deserve anything better because of the choices we have made. It is hard to look in the mirror and see despair, self-loathing, and hopelessness staring back at us. It is easier to mask the pain with a pill, a drink, or any artificial means that dulls the pain and helps us to avoid dealing with the root cause of the fear. We begin to believe the voices in our head that tell us we are unloved and unlovable. Satan wants us to feel this way and each time we feel worthless and ugly inside and out, he wins the battle he is waging on our emotional responses. In her book, Lies Women Believe: And the Truth That Sets Them Free, DeMoss (2001), reminds us that "due to our fallen condition, our feelings often have very little to do with reality. In many instances, feelings are simply not a reliable gauge of what is actually true" (p. 195). Therefore, for those who have chosen drugs, alcohol, or food to alter, mask, or escape true feelings are only running from authentic emotions of reality or truth. Instead, DeMoss tells us that reliability can come only from God and His truth. The Enemy lies to us to make us believe we have no choice but to be controlled by our negative emotions, even though we do not have to experience the negativity when we ask God to be our guide and teacher of the truth that He has given to us (p. 197).

Because God wants all of us and all of our hearts, He will help remove obstacles that interfere with our ability to turn everything over to Him. At this point it is about belief. Either you believe God is real or you do not. You cannot believe in Him when you are desperate and in trouble then turn around and not call on His wisdom when things are going well. God wants to be part of your entire life, not just when you cannot figure it out on your own. Bring Him along when you are happy and feeling like life is a blessing. After all, He is responsible for that blessing. It is a gift He has given to you. What will you give Him in return? All He wants is your devotion, praise, and a thankful heart. We do not have to do the hard things on our own, we only need to call on

Him and then wait on Him to provide all that we need. Notice, I did not say all that we *want*, but rather all that we *need*. He is fully capable of handling anything we face. Terkeurst wrote "I say yes to God because He is perfectly able to forgive me, love me, remind me, challenge me, and show me how to weather trials in ways that prove His Spirit resides in me" (2007, p. 70). What a wonderful free gift that is so easily received.

Why is it so Hard?

> We were under great pressure, far beyond our ability to endure, so that we despaired even of life. Indeed, in our hearts we felt the sentence of death. But this happened that we might not rely on ourselves but on God, who raises the dead. 2 Corinthians 1:8a-9

We all know change is hard. We also know that sometimes we are successful and sometimes not so much. There will be times when we feel that we are at a loss and not able to help ourselves. We must rely on God alone to lift us up and prevent us from self-destruction. Let us consider the importance of taking baby steps where repentance and forgiveness are involved; not because change cannot happen or that the change is not worth immediate attention, but rather because failure is painful and can knock the individual off course when success is not realized at any level. Such as, when an alcoholic shares one day of sobriety; celebrate and say thank you to God. When that single day turns into a week, celebrate again with a thankful heart. And so it goes with each little baby step. If the drinking resurfaces own up to it and share the step backward with a safe person, someone you trust to hold you accountable in love. And of course, celebrate the fact that you have someone safe to talk to about the problem. It is important to the success of making change that you find some who will not judge but who will keep expectations in tact. Additionally, it will help if you have someone who will remind you of the goals you have set and how to look first to God in all things. Without encouragement along the way, the individual seeking help will return to the addiction as a source of relief rather than going to a place where they are safe from judgment, criticism, and rejection. So, why is it so hard? Because the sin is not part of God's plan, it is not part of His hopes for you. It is hard because you have chosen the way yourself, your have made all of the decisions on your own, and you have set yourself up for failure by trying to be in charge of your own life. Instead, consider how things may be different when you involve God in each part of your life. "Don't be unrealistic about your expectations for change. It has taken nearly a lifetime of negative thinking to reach this point. It may take a long time for full healing to take place" (Hunt, 2005, p. 199).

Take time to think about the hard things you have had to do in your life. How many people were involved besides you and how were they involved? Have you ever wondered why you are so discontent with how life seems to be playing out? Of course all we need to do is take a long look in the mirror and talk to the reflection about who is really at fault? What is it you are drawn to when you feel unhappy? What seems to draw your attention instead of turning your eyes toward heaven? Life, and all of the ups and downs that comes with it, is not promised to be problem free. However, there is always an answer found in Scripture. One of my favorites is, "I can do everything through him who gives me strength" (Philippians 4:13). God does not say that if you believe in Him all things will be easy. He does not say that if we follow Christ we will never have a problem again. Instead, He promises that He will walk with us, pick us up when we fall, and give us the tools we need to be strong in Him.

Part of the issues we face that cause us to feel the pain and suffering that goes with trying to make major change in our lives is based on our own emotional health. As we mentioned before, we tend to believe what others say to and about us. We fall into the trap of negativity and feel we are worthless and that it is just too difficult and too much work to give up a lifetime of poor decisions and bad habits. We are emotionally drained and the energy needed to fulfill God's plan for us is too hard to even begin to approach. Where is your emotional health? Do negative thoughts consume your days and worry your nights? Omartian shared,

> My definition of emotional health is having total peace about who you are, what you're doing, and where you're going, both individually and in relationship to those around you. In other words, it's feeling totally at peace about the past, present, and future of your life. It is knowing that you're in line with God's ultimate purpose for you and being fulfilled in that. When you have that kind of peace and you no longer live in emotional agony, then you are a success. (p. 3)

To succeed in making the difficult changes, it may mean you are called to remove yourself from people or situations that draw you into the realm of captivity that you are trying to change in your life. Such changes will be part of the steps needed to receive the forgiveness you seek from God's promised grace and mercy. Perhaps it is time to make some hard choices; change jobs, change living conditions, change friendships, avoid places where triggers set you off into old habits, ask for forgiveness from those you have hurt and from God, etc. Of course it may not be possible to make every needed change at the same time, but it also may be necessary to take that first step away from the dark and move into the light.

Discussion Points

Making change is difficult regardless of whether it is a small or a large change that we need to address. We have discussed a great deal about repentance and forgiveness. The two go hand in hand and we have learned that to receive God's forgiveness we must first repent of the sin of which has been instrumental in our daily living. Think about the following questions as beginning points to address the needed change and how to move toward repentance followed by forgiveness.

a. What is the most difficult thing you do every day? Why?

b. Who is the most challenging person in your life?

c. What frightens you most when you think about giving up something that has held you captive?

d. Who do you consider to be a *safe* person for sharing concerns or asking questions?

e. How do you feel when you know you made a poor decision? How do you feel when things turn out well?

f. What is the first thing you can do to rectify a problem you caused?

g. What do you need to do first to begin the change process?

h. What does it mean to lay your sin at the foot of the cross?

Prayer

Dear Lord, thank You for being with us in this room today. Thank You for being only a whisper away any time we need You. Help us to call on You as we make decisions that will impact our life and that of our family. Remind us daily that You are the only one who knows what is best for us. We know You judge our actions and we know You want only the best for us. Help us to acknowledge your spirit and recognize the need to call on You before making choices that are not good for us. Please walk with us as we continue to look at the sin in our lives and show us the first steps we need to make in order to repent and receive Your forgiveness. It is in Your son's name that we ask, Amen.

<u>Leader Notes</u>: At this point in my sessions, I discuss the idea of defining the problem, or root cause of the issue each women is experiencing. It is important to begin with a definition of what they actually need to repent in order to move into forgiveness. Brown identified this step as a *prerequisite to recovery* (1992). He continues with "vague anxiety without definition of its source will simply wipe you out" (p. 94). Helping each women identify what they feel they need to repent will vacillate from great detail to blank stares. You will find some are not ready to put a finger on what is the cause of their decisions to move into negative life styles. Be patient, it all depends on how much work each person has done on the problem. Some will have been in previous groups, a twelve-step program, or even rehab centers. The point is do not expect every individual to be at the same place in their journey toward recovery. Additionally, as you discuss ownership of the sin, remind them that what was done to them by another person is not their fault, especially if a childhood incident. However, what they do with the issue and how they respond is their own responsibility.

Negative Interference

Therefore, since we are surrounded by such a great cloud of witnesses, let us throw off everything that hinders and the sin that so easily entangles, and let us run with perseverance the race marked out for us. Hebrews 12:1

As we mentioned earlier, negativity may be a major part of what each of us experiences from family and friends. It is likely there are times when we feel no one is on our side and that those who are supposed to care for us most have abandoned us physically and/or emotionally. A feeling of abandonment can lead to discouragement and depression. Levels of discouragement are different for each individual and very real to the person swallowed by depression. Where do we turn when the world seems so dark and we feel so alone? Dr. Jeremiah states, "it takes diligent faith to live above discouragement" (2001, p. 22). The Life Application Bible provides a definition of discouragement as "to hinder; to deprive of courage or hope" (2005, NIV, p. 2322). There are many things in a person's life that can lead to loss of courage or hope, much of which is from our own doing. When we are discouraged it is easy to fall into old habits that seemed, at the time, to help us forget the pain of discouragement. We need to realize that any negative thought we have about ourselves will impact the roles we have in life; friend, spouse, parent, sibling, etc. Each of the people we interact with will be touched in some way by what we say and do. Can you honestly say you give your best to the people you care about or are you consumed with negativity about yourself and your life to the point of destroying healthy relationships?

All of us are made in God's image and yet we are all one of a kind. He does did not allow you to be born without having a plan for you. He looks upon you as His child and is proud of His creation. Max Lucado once wrote; "You aren't an accident. You weren't massed produced. You aren't an assembly-line product. You were deliberately planned, specifically gifted, and lovingly positioned on this earth by the Master Craftsman" (1998, p. 57). Because Satan is in the world, ugly things happen and you may find yourself discouraged or depressed. You may be someone who was mistreated in horrible ways through no fault of your own. What has happened *to you*, is never your fault, but what you do with it is your call. How you handle the results, the attitude you develop, the habits you fall into, or the hurts you cause others is your doing alone. God wants to help you with the ugliness that has been done to you and He wants to help you become stronger and use the hurt to develop a heart for others who experience trauma in their lives that perhaps only you can understand.

Discussion Points

The following questions can be used as part of a group discussion. However, some questions may be very difficult for participants to speak to in public. I never force anyone to respond if they are uncomfortable. I do encourage each person to take time to reflect on each question and think about how they would answer.

a. How does it feel to face negative responses from those you love when you try to share a concern about your addiction/problem?

b. What does the difference between asking for forgiveness and actually repenting mean to you?

c. What makes repenting difficult in your situation?

d. What temptations or coercions do you face that impedes your ability to fully repent?

e. When does negative self-talk and behavior get in the way of your relationships?

f. Where do you feel most safe to share successes and failures?

g. When do you feel most like a failure? When do you feel most successful?

h. Describe how you would approach repentance in your prayer life?

Prayer

Dear Heavenly Father, we struggle so often with finding a way to fully repent of our sins. We know You forgive us and love us as we turn to You for forgiveness. Please help us to understand and apply repentance as part of our spiritual growth and understanding. Help us to fully embrace the repenting or the sins You have forgiven. Help us to recognize temptations and coercions that get in the way of our success and remind us daily that we were not born as an accident but as part of Your plan and purpose. In Jesus' name, Amen.

From Negative to Positive

> Therefore we do not lose heart. Though outwardly we
> are wasting away, yet inwardly we are being renewed
> day by day. 2 Corinthians 4:16

In order to fully repent means to do away with the negatives that produce barriers toward true repentance. Some such negatives include listening to the voices that continue to convince you that you are not worthy of love, spending time with people who do not have your best interest at heart, going to places where you fall into a trap of negative behaviors, allowing the evil that consumes you to have full control. After all, when sin has taken complete control, then to repent means to do away with the negativity that is leading you to continue the sin. There are really two categories of people: those who follow the dark and those who follow the light. Another way to express this idea is that some people choose to be controlled by their sinful nature and others choose to follow Christ. Romans 8:5 states, "Those who live according to the sinful nature have their minds set on what that nature desires; but those who live in accordance with the Spirit have their minds set on what the Spirit desires." It all becomes a tug-of-war against the dark and the light. There is much power in our sinful nature; after all it is controlled by how much power we give to the negative elements (Satan) in our lives. However, there is more power in what God can and wants to do for us. He is greater than Satan or any other form of negativity, but we must give that power to

God on our behalf. He will not intervene in our sin if we do not want Him involved. And yet all we have to do is ask. Ask Him to give us the strength we need to say no to the negativity in our lives and yes to His all-consuming love.

Becoming positive in a time when we feel defeated is not an easy task. Meyer, in her book Battlefield of the Mind (2011) explains, "Positive minds produce positive lives. Negative minds produce negative lives. Positive thoughts are always full of faith and hope. Negative thoughts are always full of fear and doubt" (p. 39). For some people the idea of thinking positively means having hope and hope seems futile when disappointment has been the norm (p. 39). Choosing to look to the positive through God's promises seems fruitless at times because God can seem very distant when we are struggling with negativity. Living a life of negativity and sin can destroy a relationship between man and God. When the negative consumes and destroys, repentance will need to be part of the healing process. Repentance begins with accepting the responsibility of the sin and then realizing the path to redemption is about following the plans God has provided for you. The path to God's plan is about finding the positive life He wants for you. The Bible tells us a great deal about the work of Paul and his many trials, sufferings, and distress he felt as he worked hard to bring the message of Christ to unbelievers. His concentration of the goals he had to receive his rewards in heaven was much of what kept him going. His faith was strong and he had no doubts that what Jesus preached was indeed the ultimate truth. This is a lesson for all of us. It is easy to give into the pain and focus on the negativity rather than holding tight to our faith and concentrate on the ultimate goal. For now, we seek goals that are achievable in the short term that will lead to the final goal of being a part of God's holy kingdom.

> Therefore we do not lose heart. Though outwardly we
> are wasting away, yet inwardly we are being renewed
> day by day. For our light and momentary troubles are
> achieving for us an eternal glory that far outweighs
> them all. So we fix our eyes not on what is seen, but
> on what is unseen. For what is seen is temporary, but
> what is unseen is eternal. (2 Corinthians 4:18)

A major part of finding the positive in life to overcome the
negative is in how we obtain joy. Once repentance has been
experienced, joy will well up within your soul to convict you to
move toward asking for forgiveness. Joy is a deep emotion that
seems to be a part of everything around us when it is cultivated
through the love of Christ. Joy is not one thing but many feelings
and experiences that bring inner peace and love within our
hearts. It is part of the desire to continue in the direction that
leads to forgiveness and new beginnings. You either choose joy
or you do not. It is your call. Thomas writes, "God promises
that His followers will 'ever sing for joy.' I think that promise
is supposed to shape almost everything we do while we're here"
(2011, p. 61). This author reminds us that God made the promise
of joy and we know He does not promise what He does not
intend to fulfill. However, we have the responsibility to use
the gifts He has given to us so that we may move toward joy
and way from those things that separate us from Him. "Every
day is obviously not filled with joyful circumstances or joyful
relationships, and yet we can still have a deep, soul-joy. It's a
promise" (p. 61). Take the promise, as it is intended, and allow
it to help you orchestrate the plans you have each day. How can
you use this promise to make decisions, build relationships, and
walk through your daily activities?

Discussion Points

Thomas (2011) wrote, "The first step toward a life of joy is to become a follower of Jesus Christ. The second step is to stay with Jesus, growing and learning what it means to be a Christian" (p. 47). She continues to explain that joy comes when we choose to live what we believe. Consider the following questions as you think more about joy.

a. What does the Thomas quote mean to you? How do you live what you believe?

b. Write a personal definition of repentance:

c. Write a personal definition of joy:

d. What do you need to do to begin removing the negativity in your life and working toward the positive?

Prayer

Heavenly Father, we know that repentance is a part of our ability to be forgiven by You for all of the things we have done to keep negativity in our lives. We realize that You want only joy for us and You are there to help us when we fail. Lord, help us to see You in all things and to reach out to Your love as a means to meet personal goals that include You. We ask You to show us the way to the light as we turn from the darkness and begin our journey to full repentance. We know it is hard, Lord, and we know You will be with us when things are difficult and all we have to do is ask. Bring us joy each day to remind us that we are learning what it means to follow You. In Jesus' name we pray, Amen

Conclusion

Perhaps, repentance is the most difficult step to take toward redemption. Once we are consumed by a life altering habit or debilitating sinful action, it is one thing to recognize and accept we need to make a change, but to continue in the right direction and throw away old habits can be a struggle to manage. Lutzer wrote about the <u>Seven Snares of the Enemy</u> and in his book he stated, "Christ died not only that we might be forgiven, but also that we might be delivered from the power of sin" (2001, p. 204). Repentance sounds hard, but it can be accomplished through diligence and dedication for listening to God's voice. As written by Anton, "He [God] has the answers you seek so that you may know how to repent. You will return to him. You will be refreshed" (2005, p, 15). Take heart in knowing that God does not give up on us. He wants to draw us closer to Him and will walk with us as we fight to repent and return to Him. God shows us through the work of Paul how to find joy in what we do to live in the light and turn from darkness as we move away from the negativity of sin.

CHAPTER 5

Asking for Forgiveness:
Request

Who can discern his errors? Forgive my hidden faults.
Psalm 19:12

Then David said to God, "I have sinned greatly by doing
this. Now, I beg you, take away the guilt of your servant.
I have done a very foolish thing." 1 Chronicles 21:8

Asking for forgiveness is not an easy thing to do. It means owning up to an infraction of some kind and then be repentant for it. It means to humble oneself and admit to failing at some level, possibly hurting someone we love very much. God offers us the opportunity to seek repentance and then request His forgiveness any time we need it. When we are honest and genuine in our *request*, He is ready and willing to hear us and forgive us. His desire to forgive our sinful ways is part of the grace and mercy He offers unfailingly to His children. The ability to forgive is open to we humans as well; not only may we ask someone to forgive us but we may also provide forgiveness to another. The process of forgiveness is, in part, how we relate to those we care about and how we heal from past hurts.

Before we discuss God's love and forgiveness for His children, let's begin with a brief discussion about the need to ask forgiveness from someone in our personal lives. Think about the difference between apologizing and asking for forgiveness (Shapiro, 2010). There is a distinct difference and that difference will determine if forgiveness is genuine. In most cases, those who are living with choices that have resulted in family separation will find it difficult to ask for forgiveness. They may have already apologized for causing the problem but saying "I am sorry" is not enough to help move toward a healthy relationship. The offender must also ask if the person can forgive them for (insert offense). Identify and name the offense to show a true understanding of the magnitude of what was done and to ensure both people are looking at the same issues (Shapiro). This means there is a need to humble oneself in presentation of the request for forgiveness. An open discussion can ensue after each person is able to recognize a need to reconcile (More about reconciliation will be discussed in Chapter 7). This principle of humbling oneself and speaking to the offense is exactly what we need to do when asking God to forgive us. Be specific as you request His forgiveness.

Placing Blame

> Who will bring any charge against those whom God
> has chosen? It is God who justifies. Romans 8:33

In addition to asking to be forgiven by God or by those we have hurt, we will always find a time when we need to forgive those who have hurt us. It means looking at the causes and events that have led to the issue causing pain and suffering. Such as, when we dig deeper into the causes of an addiction or negative life style, it is easy to fall into the trap of blaming others: My mother never showed me love, my father molested me, we were poor, people were prejudice against my race, my husband had an affair, etc. Even though awful things can happen to any of us, moving away from blame and learning to forgive is the only way to fully recover from the offense that was brought against our will. When something happens to us, especially as children, it is not unlikely we feel a need to be vindicated in some way. We want the offender to suffer, too. Somehow we feel justified and begin to rationalize as to why we are the mess we have become. After all, horrible things were done to us. One of the most difficult emotional shifts for anyone is to move past the blame and work toward forgiving the offender. God calls us to forgive our enemies so that we can then be forgiven; "For if you forgive men when they sin against you, your heavenly Father will also forgive you. But if you do not forgive men their sins, your Father will not forgive your sins" (Matthew 6:14-15). No one suggests this is an easy task. Meyer (2005) wrote:

> These instructions are not easy to follow. Obviously it is impossible to do so unless we choose to press past our feelings, yes, we must *press*. We must make an effort to forgive and to let go of anger. It almost seems unfair of God even to ask us to do such a thing. If you want to know the truth, I actually feel this is one of the most difficult things God asks of us. It is hard, but not impossible. The Lord never requires us to do anything without giving us the ability to do it. We may not want to forgive, but we are able to do so with God's help. (p. 140)

Placing blame does not make the offense disappear. In fact, it often just reopens the old wound over and over again. Forgiving instead of placing blame will free you up to move on and heal your emotional trauma. "The most important thing to remember about forgiveness is that forgiveness doesn't make the other person right: it makes you free" (Omartian, 2003, p. 24). Once you can honestly say you forgive the offender, then you are ready to emotionally move on. I am not suggesting this is an easy process or an overnight fix, but I do know that in time, with prayer and diligence, you can forgive and feel the freedom offered to you from releasing the pain and hatred that has been part of your heart for so long.

According to the above Scripture we are called to have compassion for one another. This is pretty easy to do when it means caring for the elderly grandmother we have always loved. It is not hard at all to have compassion for an abandoned child that needs a loving adult to care for them. Helping a wheelchair bound person open a door is simple compassion any of us are willing to do. But, showing compassion for someone who has been hurtful or neglectful is an entirely different challenge. Where do we get the strength to overlook the hurt, forgive them for causing the hurt or neglecting the needs we have? How can we be expected to just brush it all aside and forgive? The answer falls in the words of Jesus found in Matthew 6:15 "but if you do not forgive men their sins, your Father will not forgive your sins." Ouch, I am supposed to be Christ-like and forgive? I admit this is one very difficult thing for me to be able to do. I have been hurt deeply by the people I love the most. I have shed buckets of tears over a broken heart due to abandonment, physical abuse, and broken promises. Those things never leave me; they are part of the fabric of my personality. However, I have made a choice to forgive what was done *to* me, because of what Christ did *for* me.

Although we are commanded to forgive, I do not believe God expects us to forget the hurt. In fact, Scripture tells us that He uses what we are subjected to in order to make us stronger and better for His kingdom. Kendall (2002) wrote, "totally forgiving someone doesn't necessarily mean we will want to spend our vacation with him or her, but it does mean that we release the bitterness in our hearts concerning what they have done" (p. 8). Since we know how the pain of being held captive by our negative choices affects our physical as well as emotional well-being, to release the bitterness will serve to help make us healthier over time. The following list is provided in Kendall's book, Total Forgiveness, and explains what forgiving is NOT.

It is not:

> Approval of what they did.
> Excusing what they did.
> Justifying what they did
> Pardoning what they did
> Reconciling
> Denying what they did
> Blindness to what they did
> Forgetting what they did
> Refusing to take the wrong seriously
> Pretending we are not hurt

"Total forgiveness is a choice. It is not a feeling—at least at first—but is rather an act of the will" (p. 21).

Forgiving others for what they have done to hurt us is very difficult and may even seem impossible. It takes putting aside the offense and forgiving the action committed by the person. As we learned it does not mean you forget what happened or to become a part of the offender's life. It does mean that in order to feel peace you must put the sin of another into the hands of God. He is the one who will judge and deal with any needed punishment.

Discussion Points

God requires that we forgive those we love and those who have hurt us. In Scripture we find support for this idea as follows in the activity below. Use the following Scriptures to grasp God's plan for forgiveness. List three things that you could do to begin the process of asking someone to forgive you. Then list three things that you can do to begin the process of forgiving someone who has hurt you:

- Then David said to God, "I have sinned greatly by doing this. Now, I beg you, take away the guilt of your servant. I have done a very foolish thing." 1 Chronicles 21:8
- Who can discern his errors? Forgive my hidden faults. Psalm 19:12
- Brothers, I do not consider myself yet to have taken hold of it. But one thing I do: Forgetting what is behind and straining toward what is ahead. Philippians 3:13

  Three things I can do to begin the process of asking someone to forgive me:
  1.

  2.

  3.

- Be kind and compassionate to one another, forgiving each other, just as in Christ God forgave you. Ephesians 4:32
- Bear with each other and forgive whatever grievances you may have against one another. Forgive as the Lord forgave you. Colossians 3:13
- Then Peter came to Jesus and asked, "Lord how many times shall I forgive my brother when he sins against me? Up to seven times?" Jesus answered, "I tell you, not seven times, but seventy-seven times." Matthew 18:21-22

Three things I can do to begin the process of forgiving someone who has hurt me:

1.

2.

3.

Leader Notes: In this chapter, we discussed hurts, failures, accusations, blame, and much more. I have found that some women who are in conflict with another individual will find difficulty in how they manifest the pain involved. Some will be openly angry and raise their voice while claiming to *never forgive or forget* what the other person has done to them. Some women will cry and become very emotional as hurts are revealed, perhaps for the first time in public. Others will become very quiet and not want to discuss the issues that have caused the separation. The point is that each person will respond differently to a personal experience that has destroyed a relationship. You will find at times that the conflict with family and friends can lead to a broken relationship with God as it is directly related to the failed human relationship.

Prayer

Dear Lord, thank You for your undying love for us and for Your promise to forgive us when we fail You. We know we are fragile in our abilities to forgive those who have hurt us in any way. We ask that You help heal our hearts and help us to look beyond the destructiveness of blaming. Help us to take responsibility where it is due and to learn to forgive others and ourselves as we also learn to ask for forgiveness from those we have harmed in some way. In Your name we pray, Amen

Feeling Loved and Forgiven by God

> He sends from heaven and saves me, rebuking those who hotly pursue me; God sends his love and his faithfulness. Psalm 57:3

How many times have you said things like, *I just love springtime,* or *I love to sing,* perhaps you have said, *I love chocolate and just can't do without it?* Yes, me, too, I honestly believe I *love* chocolate or at least how chocolate makes me feel. It is interesting that we use the word *love* so freely within our daily activities but we do not stop to realize just how much God loves us nor do we think about how to honestly fall in love with Him. The Bible teaches love as eternal and unconditional, at least by our loving Heavenly Father. What does that mean for us? How do we fall completely in love with Jesus unless we are willing to give all of ourselves to Him? What do we need to do to receive this eternal unconditional love and forgiveness? Dr. Jeremiah suggests that:

God's love doesn't depend on how well we love Him back. It doesn't depend upon whether or not we let go. We don't earn it, deserve it, or maintain it. Yet His love is wrapped around us reinforced by His promises. It holds us perfectly and permanently. We may slip and fall, but we are not lost. (2012, pp. 202-203)

God showed His love for us in the most profound way possible as proven in one of the most important verses in the Bible, if not THE most important. This verse expresses how much God loves us; "For God so loved the world that he gave his one and only Son, that whoever believes in him shall not perish but have eternal life" (John 3:16). The Scripture shows us that God was willing to give up the most important thing to Him, his son, just to show us how much we are loved by Him. Jesus is often spoken of as the Lamb of God, meaning he was the true and last sacrifice designed by God. The death of Jesus represented full forgiveness for all of the sin in the world past and present, for those who followed Him and believed in God's love and forgiveness. From the moment of Christ's death and resurrection mankind began to live under the new covenant, that which provides everlasting hope and promise of being able to go to Jesus and ask for forgiveness. He was the final sacrifice, which according to Scripture, makes us worthy to go to God through His son instead of through a priest or an animal sacrifice as found in Old Testament history (Life Application Bible, NIV, 2005, p. 1591). The Life Application Bible continues to explain that:

Rather than an unblemished lamb slain on the alter, the perfect Lamb of God was slain on the cross, a sinless sacrifice so that our sins could be forgiven once and for all. All those who believe in Christ receive that forgiveness. (p. 1591)

Discussion Points

Use John 3:16 to discuss the implications of forgiveness for us today.

a. Why do you believe Jesus is often described as the Lamb of God?

b. What does it mean we will not perish if we believe in Him, but rather have eternal life?

c. As shared earlier in the information from Dr. David Jeremiah, how does 3:16 illustrate what Dr. Jeremiah explained when he wrote, "God's love doesn't depend on how well we love Him back. It doesn't depend upon whether or not we let go. We don't earn it, deserve it, or maintain it. Yet His love is wrapped around us reinforced by His promises. It holds us perfectly and permanently. We may slip and fall, but we are not lost?"

d. How does this love from God show us we are also worthy of forgiveness?

Read the following Scripture and discuss what it means based on John 3:16:

- For God did not send his Son into the world to condemn the world, but to save the world through him. John 3:17

> a. What understanding do you have regarding this Scripture as related to the love and forgiveness we receive from God?
>
> b. Who is *the world?*
>
> c. How can the world be *saved through Him?*

Leader Notes: It may be worthwhile to provide some background on the work of Christ and His disciples depending on how much biblical background the women in the group have. I have worked with some who have had teaching from the Bible previously and some who have not been exposed to the Bible in any form. It may be helpful to review the principles of sacrifice found in the Old Testament and compare that practice to the crucifixion of Jesus.

Prayer

Our Heavenly Father, thank You for giving us Your son by sacrificing Him to show the world that we are forgiven. We know that all we have to do is to come to You and ask that You forgive that which we have done to shame ourselves and disappoint You. Father, we know You have given the world Your greatest love through Your son. We are not worthy and continue to fail, but we ask that You show us each day how to move away from that failure and learn to listen for Your voice so that we humble ourselves to Your purpose. Thank You for Your son, Jesus Christ, and thank You for not throwing us away with lost patience as we struggle to fully heal from fear and sin that has resulted in sadness and pain. We love You, Lord, and trust You to continue to work within our spirits so that we grow more in the light with each new day. In the name of Jesus, Amen.

Worthy to be Loved

> Are not two sparrows sold for a penny? Yet not one of them will fall to the ground apart from the will of you Father. And even the very hairs of your head are all numbered. So don't be afraid; you are worth more than many sparrows. Matthew 10:29-31

Forgiving is difficult on several levels but in order to forgive yourself or others, it is imperative to understand that you are worth it. Do not let a poor self-image get in the way. Do not believe the lies that you are not worthy of love, from God or anyone else. The belief that you are unworthy can cause you to want to wilt away and not address the problems that cause you so much pain. It is not uncommon to feel a need to hide from God because we feel unworthy of His love. Thankfully, there is no way to hide because He is omnipotent and omniscient. This means He knows all and can do all. Therefore, there is no hiding from Him and He is ready to embrace you just for the asking. To fully understand the purity of God's Word is not always simple when we feel we are unworthy of His love, but isn't it amazing to know that no matter what has happened, the sun continues to shine on the just and the unjust, as the rain also falls on those who sin and those who do not? We are equal in God's eyes. There are no distinctions between those He chooses to love because He loves us all! "God disputes the notion that his children are unworthy despite sin and shame" (Pastor Hal Shrader, personal communication, March 3, 2013). And because we live in a fractured world among human beings, suffering will continue to happen to all of us. No one is exempt from living a normal human life, which does include suffering, pain, sadness, and loss. In addition, it is not uncommon for some of us to have experienced being made to feel unworthy. It is equally common to be told we, personally, are not equal in the eyes of all people and therefore we are not equal in the eyes of God. The difference is that God created us for His personal plan. He watches over us with loving eyes that do not condemn or expect failure. We were created by love, to be loved, and to give love.

Have you ever heard the saying *love conquers all*? If this refers to God's love for us, then most certainly the statement fits. However, if it refers to human nature, then perhaps we need to think about it first. Such as, what is love exactly? In my family, love often is directly related to hospitality, which includes food and fellowship. I have friends who show love by providing their children with every new technological gadget on the market. And, I have acquaintances who have taught their children that good grades and doing chores is a great way to receive love. Each of these examples fall directly into the realm of conditional love, not at all what God calls us to do. Love from God, through His son Jesus Christ, is completely unconditional. There is absolutely nothing that must be done in order to earn the love of our Heavenly Father. With this unconditional love is the offer to forgive us because He loves us so much. And all we have to do is believe in Him and ask.

We have thought about unconditional love previously through work done by Dr. David Jeremiah, but for the purpose of continuing the relevance of God's love for us and His willingness to forgive, I wanted to revisit the principles of unconditional love briefly here although a deeper discussion will be presented later in this chapter. We know that forgiveness happens directly following repentance, and we know that we must first repent in order to ask for forgiveness. Perhaps part of our dedication to following God's offer of unconditional love is to first make our sins known to Him. Yes, He already knows what we did and He loves us anyway. He knows our hearts and He knows how we struggle with facing the evil in our lives. It is not easy to own up to the sins we have committed. Anton reminds us "sin doesn't happen in general, it happens in specifics" (2005, p. 97). So to better cleanse our thoughts, our hearts, and to fully own what has kept us from a close relationship with God, admit it and place it at the foot of the cross. From that action, God can see that you accept your part in the destruction of your life and the cause of your separation from Him. You can continue to put things aside and hope no one finds out about them, but God already knows. He wants you to reveal it, admit it, and ask Him to remove it from your life. To hold on to the darkness of your thoughts only draws you further from God, instead of closer. "This feeling is the dark of night; the dark of an enemy who wants nothing more than for you to be held prisoner here for the rest of your life" (Smith, 2011, p. 59). Give it to God because He loves you no matter what.

Discussion Points

Ask each person in the group to discuss the following questions about feeling loved by those important to them.

a. What does love feel like, look like, and behave like in your own life?

b. How do you show love to others and how do they respond?

c. Distinguish between actions vs. tangibles as offerings of love.

d. Who is the easiest person in your life to love unconditionally? Who in your own life loves you unconditionally and how do you know?

e. What steps do we need to take to fully understand and accept the idea of God's unconditional love?

f. Because it is evident that we cannot earn God's love or even refuse it, how can we reach out and embrace it with a full understanding that God created us to love and be loved?

g. When have you felt most loved by God? How did the experience compare to the love you felt from your earthly parents?

h. What voices or behaviors are keeping you from seeing you the way God sees you?

i. What steps do you need to take to move toward God's plan for your life?

Prayer

Heavenly Father, we are learning so much about the love You have for us and how we are to love others in Your name. Help us to realize that love is about inner peace and trust between those we love and ourselves. Remind us of the joy we can feel when we are forgiven and when we are able to forgive others. We know You are the ultimate example of unconditional love and we ask for Your guidance as we learn how to love unconditionally. We realize not every person in our lives is lovable and that there are times when we also are not lovable, but help us remember that Your love never fails. Thank You for allowing us to be part of Your family and thank You for showing us what true love can be. We know we fail at times, but we ask for Your continued message of love that we receive from the people you place in our path. Thank You, Jesus, for being all that You are to us. In Your name we pray, Amen.

Emotional Barriers

> The Lord is close to the broken hearted and saves those
> who are crushed in spirit. Psalm 34:18

This next section is dedicated to illustrating those things that get in the way of emotional healing as we strive to draw nearer to God. In order to fully experience a feeling of forgiveness, we will now look at things that create barriers or block our understanding and development, as we grow closer to God. Because we strive to hear His voice and learn to remove ourselves from those things in life that lead to emotional captivity, we want to review areas of our inner thoughts and behaviors that may be instrumental in our failing to succeed. It should be understood that some of the topics that follow are areas that may need the help of a medical professional. I do not claim to understand the physical causes of mental illness or weakness. If you feel a need to seek medical help, I suggest you locate a doctor who you feel is a Godly person and able to help you correct any physical issue you may be experiencing. For the purpose of this study, we will talk about how our emotions play a significant part in our relationship with God and how that relationship can be strengthened. Areas covered will include, depression, seeking approval, guilt and shame, and anger.

Depression

> I am feeble and utterly crushed; I groan in anguish of
> heart. Psalm 38:8

A common issue that can get in the way of feeling forgiven is that of depression that often includes feelings of hopelessness and discouragement. It is not uncommon to let negativity consume us until we can no longer face others or ourselves. Life becomes unbearable and the road to recovery seems rocky and all uphill. You become fatigued to the point of not wanting to get out of bed each day. Sometimes when you are in a crowd, you feel very alone. It seems everything is going on around you and you are not a part of the activity. However, although difficult, there is an answer and hope for a brighter day ahead. Omartian, in her book Lord I Want to be Whole (2000), writes:

> If you are depressed, you probably have accepted a lie as the truth—usually a lie about yourself: 'You're a failure. You're no good. You won't make it. You're ugly.' But all of this is a direct opposition to Scripture, which says you have special gifts and talents. The fact that the world isn't recognizing your gifts at this moment doesn't mean they aren't there or that you are worthless. Dispel lies with the truth of God's Word. (p. 154)

It is true that depression is often a result of unresolved issues and can affect us emotionally and/or physically. DeMoss explained that the root cause of the depression should be addressed to avoid "creating very real physical and emotional problems" (p. 205). She continues with "when we fail to see God's hand in our circumstance or when we contend with Him over His choices for our lives, we become candidates for emotional and spiritual depression" (p. 206). Because depression can be a physiological issue as well as an emotional problem, it may be necessary to seek medical help, but it also may be a situation whereby you are being called to look at your spiritual life as a means for healing.

Depression can cause one to respond to others with defensive attitudes. It is hard to face failures and flaws and own up to the areas in your life that cause you embarrassment or heartache. When you find yourself to be the reason for another person's pain, whether your child, your spouse, your parent, or your friends, it can be difficult to accept the ownership without justifying or explaining away your behavior. Depression tends to cause us to look at life through a negative lens and leads us to assume negative intentions from those around us. "Confident people can listen objectively to another point of view; they can pray about what is said and either receive or reject it according to what God places in their heart" (Meyer, 2005, p. 136). How then do those with depression find the confidence to take criticism in a positive well-meaning light? The good news is that there is hope. You do not need to live in a depressive state of mind. Although I do not claim that it is easy, I do know that devoting yourself completely to learning more about God's love for you and acting on the principles of forgiveness, redemption, and reconciliation, you will find peace. The following paragraph comes from the book Approval Addiction (2005) and speaks to the things in our lives that can cause elements of depression. Read the words and determine how you fit within the perspective regarding anything causing you to feel depressed.

> No matter what happens in our life, if we will keep praying and trusting God, keep loving Him and walking in His will to the best of our ability, He will cause everything to work out for good. Whatever happened to us in the past may not have been good in and of itself, and it may have lead to a struggle with acceptance and desire for approval, but because God is good, He can take a very difficult and painful thing and cause it to work out for our good and the good of others. (Meyer, pp. 231-232)

Discussion Points

The following Scriptures were chosen to look at how depression can be conquered through God's Word to us. Read each Scripture and discuss the implications for working through depression that may be causing a barrier that keeps you from feeling forgiven.

- When I said, "My foot is slipping," your love, O Lord, supported me. When anxiety was great within me, your consolation brought joy to my soul. Psalm 94:18-19
- The righteous cry out and the Lord hears them; he delivers them from all their troubles. The Lord is close to the brokenhearted and saves those who are crushed in spirit. Psalm 34:17-18
- But those who hope in the Lord will renew their strength. They will soar on wings like eagles, they will run and not grow weary, they will walk and not be faint. Isaiah 40:31

Read all three of the Scriptures above and number them one through three with one being the Scripture that speaks to you most personally. Discuss the following questions as related to these three verses.

a. Share which verse spoke most closely to your feelings. Highlight the words that speak loudest to your heart.

b. What do you feel is the most difficult thing you will need to do in order to feel God will pull you up from your despair or depression?

c. When do you feel most depressed about your situation?

d. When do you feel most likely to believe you can work through the depression?

e. What do you do to avoid feeling the burden of depression?

f. Which of the above Scriptures seem to give you the most hope? Why?

Prayer

Thank You, Father, for being here in our presence. We praise Your name in all things and are thankful that You keep Your promises and help us to know that we can come to You and ask for Your forgiveness when we fail. We praise Your name in all things and especially thank You at this moment for the opportunity to ask for forgiveness and to know You will forgive willingly and remember it no more as part of the promise of Your love for us. We ask for guidance and direction as we learn to remove the negative voices and to focus on the perfect plan You have for us. Help us to not be discouraged and to fight any depression that is affecting our lives by turning to You for the answers and support we seek. In Jesus' name, Amen.

Leader Notes: Not all women will feel they are living with depression. It may be helpful to discuss some of the stories about David and all of his sorrow as he wrote the Psalms asking for God's help. These stories can be used as examples and compare them to situations of people you know. If you feel any of the women are severely depressed, be sure to recommend biblical counseling or medical help. This may be one of the areas where you will want to have contact information available to share with anyone showing interest. I have also used my pastor as a resource for any of the women who felt they needed some one-on-one help in this area.

Seeking Approval

> I know, O Lord, that a man's life is not his own; it is
> not for man to direct his steps. Jeremiah 10:23

Another area that can slow us down as women is our tendency to need more approval from our loved ones than do our male counterparts. The need for approval may get in the way of moving closer to God by placing our energy on satisfying the needs of others over the plans God has for us. In her book, Approval Addiction, Meyer discusses topics such as overcoming a constant need for approval, moving away from guilt and shame, looking at being a people-pleaser, and addressing past rejection. Within her work she reminds us that;

> It may seem unreasonable to us that God would love
> us, because we look at ourselves and can find no

reason for Him to do so. We understand God with
our hearts, not with our heads. People usually need
a reason to love us and accept us but God does not.
(2005, p. 21)

From these words we can help ourselves and others seek a more
personal understanding of God as the creator and planner of
our lives. Instead of working toward complete self-interest, think
about what God may want for you. First and foremost we should
seek to gain God's approval over that of all others. But, how do
we do that? It may mean first accepting who you are as God's
child. Believe He has a plan for you that includes faith in His son,
Jesus Christ. He loves you and that love is unconditional. Think
about what you do that pleases Him and do not worry about the
approval of those around you. "Do not conform any longer to
the pattern of this world, but be transformed by the renewing of
your mind" (Romans 12:2). By looking to Christ "we don't have
to live under the pressure of acceptance by performance, followed
by a fear of failure each time our performance is less than perfect"
(Meyer, 2005, p. 5).

For many women living in crisis or being held captive by addictive
behaviors will find that they may struggle with the need to please
others as part of seeking approval. How many times have we
heard of young people trying drugs or alcohol just to *be part of
the crowd?* Concern about fitting in or being accepted can lead
a person down a path of self-destruction in the long run. As
parents, it is imperative that we guide our children to think for
themselves and to look at how to please God first in all things.
This is a difficult area for women who have been living a life with
a selfish *me first* attitude or who are *people pleasers.* Meyer suggests

we look at our motives when doing what we do. She asks us to consider the following;

- Is your heart pure?
- Are you motivated by love or by fear?
- Why are you doing it?
- Are you doing this for attention?
- Are you addressing the will of God or your own intentions?

"It is not what we do that impresses God, it is the *why* behind what we do that He is concerned with" (p. 161).

Discussion Points

Using the points found in Meyer's book, let's break down each of the topics as listed above in the following ways;

1) A constant need for approval: When we worry more about what others think of us than what God wants for us, then our attention is not placed correctly. Concerns for pleasing others does not fit into the plan God has for us as His children. When making a decision always consider what God may think rather than if you are measuring up for someone who cannot possibly love you as much as your Heavenly Father. Remember, "Our flesh seeks the approval of others, is swayed by Satan's voice of condemnation, and looks for the comfortable way out" (Terkeurst, 2007, p. 81). If you are able to put Him first in all things, you will feel more relaxed in your spirit as insecurities and fears are lessened.

a. When do you struggle most with approval from someone you care about?

b. What are you feeling physically when you are not feeling approval from others?

c. How much time do you think you spend in worry over the approval from another person?

d. What areas of your life do you struggle with most when striving for approval?

Prayer

Father God we come to You today asking for intervention as we learn to recognize the areas in our lives that may cause unhealthy relationships. We know that You love us more than anyone else could possibly love us. We thank You for that undying love and seek to know more about how we relate to those around us and learn to love them without needing constant approval. Please take the parts of our past that has led us to feel a need for approval and help us to remove the need and replace it with a healthy concept of relationship. We do not want to lose people in our lives that we love but we do recognize a need to rebuild or adjust the relationships that are not healthy. We know You approve of us because You created us for Your holy plan. Allow us to become the people You have designed us to be. In Jesus' name, Amen.

Guilt and Shame

- Your guilt is taken away and Your sin atoned for. Isaiah 6:7b
- For the worshipers would have been cleansed once for all and would no longer have felt guilty for their sins. Hebrews 10:2b

These two Scriptures are written and explained in the Life Application Bible about sacrifice as done to purify those who sinned against God. In Isaiah, we learn that he wanted to be a spokesperson on behalf of God. Isaiah knew he was not capable enough to deliver God's message to the people due to his own weaknesses. Isaiah was willing to go through a painful ritual of sacrifice (touching a hot coal to his lips) in order to show God he was willing to speak on behalf of His will. The hot coal was to signify a cleansing as a full confession of sins while submitting fully to God. "Letting God purify us may be painful, but we must be purified so that we can truly represent God, who is pure and holy" (2005, NIV, p. 1086).

The Scripture from Hebrews describes the new covenant under Jesus as the final sacrifice of man. During the Day of Atonement, sacrifices made by men caused them to relive their sins, feel guilty, and were then reminded they needed to be forgiven. However, after the death and resurrection of Christ, it is now a new covenant with God that our sins are forgiven through Christ Jesus. "When we confess a sin to him, we need never think of it again. Christ has forgiven us, and the sin no longer exists" (2005, NIV, p. 2079).

- As it is written: See, I lay in Zion a stone that causes men to stumble and a rock that makes them fall, and the one who trusts in Him will never be put to shame. Romans 9:33

The above Scripture from the Life Application Bible (NIV) (2005) refers to Jesus as the *stumbling stone*, the *rock*, and used the analogy to explain how some of the Jews were not willing to believe Christ was the Messiah. These Jews were unwilling to believe he met their particular ideas of how the Son of God should behave. This Scripture illustrates that there are still those of us who stumble over the idea of following Jesus completely; it is easier to follow the ways of the world. "He requires obedience, and many refuse to put their wills at his disposal" (p. 1898).

Moving away from guilt and shame is an important part of learning how to forgive ourselves as we move closer to God. Although we continue to remind ourselves and others that we are loved no matter what by our Heavenly Father, there are always times when Satan seems to step in to remind us of our failings and of those who have abandoned us when we needed them most. We have made unlovely choices, which seemed to chase people away when we needed them. Our disobedience to Jesus causes us to feel guilty and ashamed for the person we have become and we soon lose heart that all hope is gone. Guilt and shame are painful; they destroy self-image and lead us to hopelessness and self-loathing. This is the time to remind ourselves, and others, that God does not make mistakes in His creations. He knew before you were born what He wanted for you and He does not give up . . . ever! Meyer stated that it is not unusual for people to feel guilty when they "don't receive affirmation from the people who are supposed to love them" (p. 127). Satan works very hard to defeat our ability to move forward and know that God loves us and only He can remove our guilt and shame placed upon us from past experiences and poor decisions. Encourage each other to develop friendships with Godly people and surround yourself with those who understand how God works in our lives, being open to council as we grow closer to Him.

Being rejected by people you care about or those you are in relationship with can be hurtful and promote guilt and shame. No one likes to be rejected, left out, or ignored. It is part of our human nature to want to be included and cared about. Acceptance leads to healthier relationships when the acceptance is based on purity in love and action. "Rejection is one of Satan's favorite tools to use against people" (Meyer, 2005, p. 186). Not addressing rejection can lead to broken relationships, health problems, and emotional instability. From this area of our discussion I would like to interject that God comes in to our lives as He accepts and calls us to His purpose. Instead of blaming others for who we are or how we behave, turn to those you trust to help you find God's leading in the Word. Surround yourself with people who will care for you and not expect you to be perfect. Most importantly, embrace the idea that there is hope in Christ as you continue to learn more about His love and purpose in your life.

As we all come to terms with the information shared in this section, it becomes pertinent to include the problem of listening to the negative voices that we continue to hear in our heads. These voices are generated into our psyche based on past experiences. Allowing the voices of condemnation and criticism rule over personal thoughts of self only leads to a continuum of destruction and patterns of self deprecation. Pastor Shane Hipps called this event "those things that cause us trouble in the present; emotional, personal wars in our head" (personal communication, February 26, 2012). By learning to block out, or even remove, the negative voices that lead us away from redemption will move us closer to God. The negative voices that live among our thoughts only help to build barriers and structures that prevent us from hearing God's voice. Forgiveness comes when we first go to God with open hearts to admit our sins and shortcomings while, at the same time, trusting His purpose for us. Having faith in His undying love allows us to feel forgiven and accepted by Him.

Discussion Points

Think about the following questions and discuss how they personally relate to your life and the relationships you have with friends and family. Consider how negativity plays a part in your perceptions of others and your reactions to differing situations.

a. When someone you care about rejects you, how do you react?

b. Who do you trust to help you feel accepted as a child of God?

c. How do you mask your own rejection and how does it make you feel?

d. Where can you turn to feel accepted and to heal from past feelings of rejection?

e. When do you feel Satan is working on destroying your faith in yourself as a child of God?

f. How does guilt play a part in your relationships?

g. When do you feel most unworthy and how does it affect you physically and spiritually?

h. What can you do to help yourself break the cycle of guilt and shame?

i. If you are listening to negative voices from past experiences, how can you remove the voices and look to hear God's voice instead?

Prayer

Thank you, Father, for Your words as we learn about the difficulty of living with guilt and shame. It is such a wonderful blessing to know You can help remove the negative feelings we have from the experience of situations that cause us to be filled with guilt and shame. We know some of what has happened is not of our own doing but we ask that You help us to heal from all of it, even those things we brought on ourselves due to poor decisions. Help us to fill our hurting hearts with Your love and forgiveness so that we can overcome the pain of guilt and shame. We know You want only the best for us and we accept and hold on to Your undying love for us. Thank You for being with us at this very moment and for each moment of every day. In Your precious name we pray, Amen.

<u>Leader Notes:</u> It has been my experience that this is an area where abuse and molestation may surface. It is important to help the individual realize that such actions against them is not due to anything they did and that personal shame may be a natural feeling at this time. Very young children may feel the abuse was their fault and it can take many years, even a lifetime, to work through those feelings. If you suspect such a symptom of self-shame or depression is present due to unresolved issues, then suggest that counseling be an option to help the individual heal appropriately from the experience.

Anger

- But you, O Lord, are a compassionate and gracious God, slow to anger, abounding in love and faithfulness. Psalm 86:15
- A fool gives full vent to his anger, but a wise man keeps himself under control. Proverbs 29:11
- For as churning the milk produces butter, and as twisting the nose produces blood, so stirring up anger produces strife. Proverbs 30:33

- But I tell you that anyone who is angry with his brother will be subject to judgment. Matthew 5:22a
- In your anger do not sin: Do not let the sun go down while you are still angry, and do not give the devil a foothold. Ephesians 4:26
- My dear brothers, take note of this: Everyone should be quick to listen, slow to speak, and slow to become angry, for man's anger does not bring about the righteous life that God desires. James 1:19-20

As we continue to talk about forgiveness, perhaps we need to visit the issue of anger toward God. We all understand the need to forgive ourselves, forgive others, although very difficult, and to seek God's forgiveness as a result of our repentance. However, it is not uncommon for anyone to feel angry with God. He understands such a feeling and does not hold it against us; another one of His signs of grace. Kendall wrote about these very feelings in his book, Total Forgiveness (2002). The author points out a common feeling of mistrust of God's motives when we experience living through extremely difficult or hurtful times and we know He could intervene at any time and prevent the pain we endure. Kendall explains that it is a question of the ages when people wonder why God does not use His power to stop evil and suffering. Because we live in a fallen imperfect world, such situations will definitely be a part of our lives. But, to think God wills suffering is not a correct assumption. He does not wish pain or evil to fall upon us, his children. But because we are called to faith, we are not to question but to hold to the truth that God does have His reasons and He is with us to help us through any and all tragedy that befalls us. Kendall stated;

> God does turn evil into blessing. He causes things to
> work together for good. God did not send His Son

into the world to explain evil, but rather to save us from it and to exemplify a life of suffering. Jesus, who was and is the God-man, suffered as no one else has or ever will. One day God will clear His own name from the charge of being unjust, but in the meantime, we need to trust Him and take Him at His Word that He is just and merciful. (2002, p. 33)

I often share with those in my life that I find it fascinating how we can look back on our own history and discover how God used a situation to benefit His kingdom through us. I love looking at things that happened, good and bad, and see how the pieces are fitting together today. If we take time to review our own lives we see that it starts to make more sense than it did at the time of the event. Even though in the moment we may find ourselves fully confused as to what God is doing. Or, at times we may realize we are feeling some disappointment with how God worked things out.

Such disappointment with God can lead us to be angry with Him, which in turn can lead to other difficulties in being able to forgive others or ourselves. Focus on the fact that whatever does happen will be used for the good in the long run. One of my favorite verses states, "And we know that in all things God works for the good of those who love him, who have been called according to his purpose" (Romans 8:28). The Life Application Study Bible reminds us "God is not working to make us happy, but to fulfill his purpose . . . [Those who are called] learn to accept, not resent, pain and persecution because God is with them" (2005, p. 1895). Until we can fully, or as Kendall said, totally forgive God, we cannot expect to be able to successfully forgive others or ourselves.

Discussion Points

There was a time in the late 70s when a dear friend of mine died of an excruciating form of cancer. He was 35 years old and his family and mine spent many hours together in social and church activities. Life was so much fun and we could not have had better friends. When we found out he had terminal cancer, I became very angry with God. I could not begin to understand why this God-loving man had to go through such an awful ordeal. It did not make any sense to me or anyone else. I literally shook my fist at the heavens and yelled at God for taking away someone I loved so much and who had done all God had ever asked of Him. Thankfully, I have worked through the experience and the anger. It took some time, but God really pulled me up from the despair and anger I was feeling toward Him. All of us have had times of worry and fear when things go badly; discuss the questions below to share your own feelings and experiences.

a. Share a time when you were angry with God. How did it make you feel?

b. What is most confusing to you about God's part in suffering and evil?

c. What is the most difficult thing for you to accept as far as what you feel God is calling you to do?

d. What steps can you take to work on total forgiveness; God, yourself, others?

Prayer

We come to You at this moment, dear Father, thanking You for the time You give to us each day as we learn to come closer to You and begin the hard work necessary to make ourselves pure in Your eyes. Help us to move away from the need to feel approval from those who do not have our best interests at heart and help us to base all decisions on what is pleasing to You. We ask for strength in learning to love ourselves and to put away the shame and guilt we have felt for so long. Allow us to grow in Your presence and remove the negative voices that have crippled us and kept us from fully hearing Your loving voice. Guide us as we seek understanding how to forgive those who may have hurt us in some way as well as learn how to forgive ourselves. We ask all this in Your name, Amen.

Forgiving Yourself

Therefore, there is now no condemnation for those who are in Christ Jesus, because through Christ Jesus

the law of the Sprit of life set me free from the law of
sin and death. Romans 8:1-2

Although we touched on the concept of forgiving ourselves earlier
in this chapter, we need to look a bit deeper at what self-forgiveness
is about. One of the most difficult things for a person to master is
that of forgiving themselves. This is where grace and mercy come
into play. Dr. David Jeremiah wrote in his book God Loves You:
He Always Has-He Always Will:

> Grace and mercy lie at the foot of the cross of Christ
> for all who have chosen other than God's best. I
> implore you to give yourself the advantage of seeing
> any wrong choice in life as God sees it when it is
> confessed: as a choice that is forgiven through the
> blood of Christ. (2012, p. 40)

Because God never gives up on us and "He looks forward to the
deep satisfaction of seeing his child put to use the gifts that were
so lovingly reserved for him" (p. 41) we have the honor of using
those gifts to reach our full potential as given to us. Before we are
able to fully use our God-given gifts we will need to recognize
and request forgiveness from the One who has created us. It
appears that forgiving another person, although not easy, can be
more achievable than to fully forgive yourself, especially if you
are responsible for the pain of another person. Often a person
living with an addiction, or other self-destructive behavior, will
find they have hurt many people they love. Instead of addressing
the guilt, an addict may turn to additional use of the negative
behavior to mask the guilt they feel. In order for a person to work
toward physical and emotional healing, forgiveness may need to
be addressed. It is difficult for some to feel worthy of forgiveness

and they may fight the acceptance or ownership of the behaviors that have lead to the destruction of relationships.

Looking inside and seeing the ugliness that is dwelling within our hearts and souls can be frightening and very uncomfortable. Sometimes the blackness is there because of how we were molded by life's experiences. However, some of the darkness is there because of how we feel about ourselves. When we are responsible for hurting someone else, it can eat away at us until we face the responsibility and begin to forgive ourselves for what we have done. God already knows and has not written you off as a lost cause. He knows your heart and He knows when you are responsible for your own actions. You cannot hide from Him even though you may try to hide from yourself and from others. Hidden secrets are not going to go away, they are part of the fabric of your being, but you do not have to carry the ugliness with you. Show yourself mercy as God shows His children. Give yourself a pass on self-abuse and ask God to show you how to forgive yourself for the things you have done. He will do it and you will feel a peace that you have not felt for a very long time. Omartian said it best when she wrote:

> Emotionally wounded people often feel guilty about not being what they think they should be. Instead of beating ourselves up for that, we need to be merciful. We have to be able to say, "self, I forgive you for not being perfect, and I thank You, God, that You are right now making me into all that You created me to be." (2000, p. 25)

The following Scriptures may be useful as you consider forgiveness and the need to *request* forgiveness of our sins as part of the process of healing and redemption.

- Do not judge, and you will not be judged. Do not condemn, and you will not be condemned. Forgive, and you will be forgiven. Luke 6:37
- ... and repentance and forgiveness of sins will be preached in his name. Luke 24:47
- For he has rescued us from the dominion of darkness and brought us into the kingdom of the Son he loves, in whom we have redemption, the forgiveness of sins. Colossians 1:13-14

Discussion Points

Looking at the three Scriptures above, think about the forgiveness you seek. We all need to ask forgiveness when we fail to follow faithfully that which God has called us to do. Discuss the following questions regarding forgiveness and apply them to your own personal life.

a. Name the things you have done of which you hope to be forgiven?

b. Which is more difficult, forgiving yourself or someone else? Why?

c. Where do you feel you fall short and need forgiveness?

d. Considering the following Scripture: "If your brother sins, rebuke him, and if he repents, forgive him. If he sins against you seven times in a day, and seven times comes back to you and says, I repent, forgive him" (Luke 17:3). Why is this difficult to follow? What does it mean to rebuke someone? How does this relate to forgiving yourself?

e. What can you do to begin the process of forgiving yourself for hurting someone?

Making mistakes that cause us to fail is something we all do at some time or another. When we fail ourselves we are disgusted and look at ways to correct the error. When we fail someone else it is not as easy because now another person is involved and they can see our error and they may have been impacted in a negative way. The failure on your part may cause a break in a relationship or destroy trust so that someone you care very much about does not feel the same way about you. Now what do you do? Can you earn the trust back from the person you hurt? Can you ever forgive yourself? I have worked with women who felt they were not worthy of being forgiven. It can be very difficult to forgive yourself when those you have hurt do not let you forget what you have done. This is the time to grab a hold of the premise of God's unfailing love. He will carry you through the process of forgiveness even though there may be times when the person you have hurt chooses not to forgive. This can be very painful and yet you cannot be responsible for the actions or feelings of another person. You can pray for them and ask God to soften their heart, but ultimately you cannot force them to forgive. It may take years for the forgiveness to come to fruition or it may never happen, but the knowledge in knowing God will always forgive can bring solace to your personal pain if you will submit yourself to fully embracing His love for you.

The idea of forgiveness from others as well as from self leads us to think about unconditional love. If conditions are not placed on true relational love then why is it we find it difficult to be forgiven when we continue to fail at making needed change? I have a niece who has struggled for years with a drug addiction. When family members discuss her habit and concern for her health she often responds angrily with accusations that we, as Christians, are supposed to love unconditionally and not judge. She is right on many levels, we are not supposed to judge and we are supposed to love unconditionally. The problem, however, is in her understanding of the true meaning of unconditional love. This is a good example of identifying the behavior as part of the person instead of separate from self. Christ calls us to love, even the unlovely. He calls us to love our enemies and to bind ourselves to the love He has shown us and then pass on that love to those around us. I can certainly love my niece unconditionally, meaning loving her as God's child, as His creation. No matter what, I will always love her. She cannot do anything that will separate my love from her. I cannot however love her choices unconditionally and approve of the behavior that is destroying her as the child of God she was meant to be. Will I continue to pray for her no matter what? Yes, of course, I will also pray that God open her eyes to the addiction and how it is affecting her life. I also pray that He send someone into her life who will be able to help her see what is happening to her health and her happiness and lead her to Christ.

Discussion Points

Take some time to think about the people in your life you have hurt over time. You may have even caused harm to your own children due to your behaviors. This kind of action can lead to long-term influences on the choices your children make when they become teens or adults. As you consider the people you may have hurt in some way, begin to talk to God about how to heal your hurting heart and remove the guilt and shame you are facing. Ask for the ability to forgive yourself as you also work on asking for forgiveness from others.

a. Have you ever tried to forgive yourself for hurting someone you care about? How did it go?

b. Think about the things you have done that may have been hurtful to another person. What have you done, if anything, to rectify the hurt?

c. Are there things in your life of which you find difficult to forgive within yourself?

d. What are your thoughts about unconditional love as you understand its meaning?

e. What steps do you need to take to begin the process of forgiving yourself?

f. What steps do you need to take to begin the process of asking others for forgiveness?

g. What steps do you need to take to begin the process of asking God for forgiveness?

Prayer

Our dear Heavenly Father, we realize there is much to be forgiven and although it is difficult, we want to learn how to forgive ourselves for those things that have hurt You and others. We want to understand Your unconditional love and to receive the peace offered through forgiveness. Help us to understand fully Your promise to love and to forgive no matter what. Help us to face the uncertainty and fear involved in forgiving ourselves for those things that have not been pleasing to You. In Your son's name I pray, Amen.

Embracing God's Love

> Because your love is better than life, my lips will
> glorify you. I will praise you as long as I live, and in
> your name I will lift up my hands. Psalm 63:3-4

How often have you heard that *nothing in life is free*? This of course is true when we look at material possessions or even certain relationships. There are situations whereby people are given a roof over their head for a price that is anything but free, a price that may include exploitation and unreasonable expectations. However, the Bible is explicit on the freedom we have in accepting God's love. There is no price or threat involved. God loves us no matter what. In Romans 8:35-39 we discover this truth. It is written that,

> Yet in all these things we are more than conquerors
> through Him who loved us. For I am persuaded that
> neither death nor life, nor angels nor principalities nor
> powers, nor things present nor things to come, nor
> height nor depth, nor any other created thing, shall
> be able to separate us from the love of God which is
> in Christ Jesus our Lord.

There is no doubt that God loves us no matter how unlovable we are. The following Scriptures will allow further study of Godly love and how He applies it to each of His children. Read each verse and reflect on the meaning you gain from it. How do each of these verses relate to you personally?

- Give thanks to the Lord, for he is good; his love endures forever. 1 Chronicles 16:34
  Personal Reflection:

- Turn, O Lord, and deliver me; save me because of your unfailing love. Psalm 6:4
  Personal Reflection:

- He sends from heaven and saves me; rebuking those who hotly pursue me; God sends his love and his faithfulness. Psalm 57:3
  Personal Reflection:

-Surely goodness and love will follow me all the days of my life. Psalm 23:6
Personal Reflection:

- The Lord is compassionate and gracious, slow to anger, abounding in love. Psalm 103:8
  Personal Reflection:

- Let them give thanks to the Lord for his unfailing love and his wonderful deeds for men. Psalm 107:8
  Personal Reflection:

- Oh Israel, put your hope in the Lord, for with the Lord is unfailing love and with him is full redemption. Psalm 130:7
  Personal Reflection:

- The Lord your God is with you, he is mighty to save. He will take great delight in you, he will quiet you with his love, he will rejoice over you with singing. Zephaniah 3:17
  Personal Reflection:

- And hope does not disappoint us, because God has poured out his love into our hearts by the Holy Spirit, whom he has given us. Romans 5:5
  Personal Reflection:

- Love must be sincere. Hate what is evil; cling to what is good. Be devoted to one another in brotherly love. Romans 12:9-10
  Personal Reflection:

- Love is patient, love is kind. It does not envy, it does not boast, it is not proud. It is not rude, it is not self-seeking, it is not easily angered, it keeps no record of wrongs. Love does not delight in evil but rejoices with the truth. It always protects, always trusts, always hopes, always perseveres. 1 Corinthians 13:4-7
  Personal Reflection:

- There is no fear in love. But perfect love drives out fear, because fear has to do with punishment. The one who fears is not made perfect in love. 1 John 4:18
  Personal Reflection:

The idea of unfailing love from God's holy spirit is difficult for some to embrace. It may take some time for you to develop security in knowing that God loves you regardless of what has happened in the past. Take the time needed to think about your personal understanding of this unconditional love, however do not become discouraged if the process seems slow or unsuccessful. To *plant a seed* is of great worth so by thinking and reflecting on this idea allows you to plant a seed of understanding. Someone else in the future may be able to help cultivate and nourish the seed as you witness full growth. Just remember that God is the master gardener in your life. Working to understand the idea of forgiveness, faithfulness, and love from a Heavenly Father may not yet be fully understood or experienced, but do not give up on your spiritual growth and understanding. All answers await you within His presence and power.

Discussion Points

Use the following questions to think about love and how it affects relationships. Each question is designed to draw the participant into self-reflection and not designed to instigate blame upon past relationships.

a. What was your first experience with parental love? What did your parent do to show you love?

b. If you are a parent, what areas can you work on to enhance your child's realization that you love them? In what areas are you not as strong as you would like to be?

c. How do you feel when you experience love from a friend?

d. What experiences have you had with unconditional love?

e. What experiences have you had with finding God's love through others?

<u>Leader Notes</u>: At this point in the program, I take time to discuss love at all levels that we usually understand; parental love for children, marital love between spouses, etc. There have been times when physical love comes to surface in this section. Often I find that the women who attend my group settings are victims of sexual abuse or molestation. Some are victims of spousal abuse. Not only do these experiences affect the levels of self-esteem, they often filter into parenting styles of the women who have been violated in this manner. I have suggested in some cases for the abused to seek deeper counseling to address any trauma that may be related to unresolved issues beyond that which can be worked through in our sessions together. I make it very clear that I am not a licensed psychologist and do not claim to have the capabilities to help them with the seriousness involved in abuse issues. However, I also suggest that they find Christian counseling if at all possible. This is an area I like to have investigated so that I may offer possible names of counselors dedicated to helping women who may not have the funding to afford the needed help. Consider that the results from traumatic experiences can cause the women to feel they are not worthy of love from any source. It is important to help build and encourage them to believe in God's love for them regardless of what has happened to cause a feeling of abandonment in this area of their lives.

Prayer

Thank You, Lord, for providing beauty in love. The love You have for us is undying and unconditional and for that we give thanks. Please help us to spread Your love to others through our actions and deeds. Help us to know when someone is in need of feeling Your love through us. We pray for understanding and wisdom as we learn more about embracing the love You have for Your children. Guide us each day as we work and play among Your people. Make disciples of us as we represent the power of Your love. We ask this in Jesus' name, Amen.

Conclusion

This chapter has allowed us to look at how we *request* forgiveness in the areas where we have failed to meet God's expectations for us. Forgiveness is a gift God gives to all of His people and He wants all of us to feel His presence in that forgiveness. We need to look beyond ourselves and think about what we have done that has separated us from God's purpose and make a concerted effort to reach out to Him and request His love and understanding no matter what we have done to fall short of His plan. We have discussed the importance of forgiving ourselves as well as embracing God's forgiveness from the sins we have experienced in our daily lives. Not only is it difficult to forgive ourselves for all we have done, it is equally difficult to forgive those who have hurt us. Forgiveness may take time for those who have been deeply hurt by people they love most, but God is always with us ready to take on the pain and suffering we experience from broken relationships. He is the anchor to our soul, keeping us afloat and protecting us from drifting far away from His purpose, of which He has designed just for us.

CHAPTER 6

Breaking the Chain of Destruction: *Redemption*

Not only so, but we ourselves, who have the first fruits
of the Spirit, grown inwardly as we wait eagerly for
our adoption as sons, the redemption of our bodies.
Romans 8:23

The term redemption will be defined as "To buy back,
repurchase; to rescue (often from sin) with a ransom"
(Life Application Bible, NIV, 2005, p. 2358) and will be
looked at as the ultimate return to a positive life style that includes
God's love and acceptance. The ransom, of which the definition
speaks, refers to Christ's death on the cross. He was the final
sacrifice and was given up by God to represent our sinful nature
and to complete the forgiveness we receive from God through
His son, Jesus Christ. To fully understand a redemptive heart is
to give up a sinful nature and honor God with all of your heart,
your soul, and your mind (Deuteronomy 6:5). How is it possible
to walk away from old habits that hold us captive? Those things
that own us are not of God but rather of the world. God truly
wants you to be blessed in all things. He created you for relational
happiness so why do we fight against His purpose by allowing

that which is not of God to control our actions? When we allow the world to provide our needs, whether for physical or emotional support, we are disallowing God to do His work in us. God will not stand in your way if you choose artificial love over His love for you. He will however show you the right way to go if you give in to Him completely and trust His choices for you. It is much easier to stay with an addiction than it is to remove yourself from that which holds you in bondage and make the changes you need to be part of God's Kingdom. It takes work and sacrifice to turn away from the things that control you and to return to God's loving embrace. However, this does not mean you must do it alone, you have God on your side and He will protect your efforts by sending His people to you to help hold you accountable and give you emotional strength to move toward the light.

It is pretty obvious that you cannot change a destructive habit without help. If it were easy then addicts and alcoholics would simply decide to stop the drug or the alcohol when they wanted to. Picture yourself holding God's hand and walking side by side with Him as He guides you down the path of freedom. Hanging on to an addiction or unhealthy habit can hold you captive, which then breaks your bond with God and others. Lutzer wrote:

> This union with Christ is the basis for transforming our lifestyle and desires. Despite our struggles and failures, we must not think of ourselves as sinners or as addicts but rather as redeemed people joined to Christ for a life of spiritual freedom and personal holiness. (2001, p. 204)

What you decide now, impacts your future and the future of your children. Take care of your body, mind, and spirit by becoming strong in the Lord. He is the solution to all that tempts you to remain in Satan's grip.

Cleansing of the Soul

In the paths of the wicked lie thorns and snares,
but he who guards his soul stays far from them.
Proverbs 22:5

To demonstrate a redemptive heart, we need to think about throwing out the old and the destructive behaviors and bring on the peace and cleanliness that we gain through following Christ. We know and understand that God will forgive us of our poor decisions and hurtful behaviors. He will make us clean of the sin and provide opportunity to move in a positive healthy direction. Part of this action becomes a cleansing of our spirit: A means of purity in purpose as we continue to follow Him. In Psalms we read of David's cry of repentance to God due to his impure actions with Bathsheba and his plan to have her husband killed in order to hide his relationship with her. However, as David knew, God was well aware of his actions and yet was willing to forgive David's actions when David called out to God for the cleansing of his sins. It is important to note that even though God is true to His Word and will forgive and cleanse, He does not necessarily remove the consequences of our actions. In David's case, his family and his life were altered forever as a result of his own actions (Psalm 51:1-7). What then does this mean for us today? God continues to forgive and to cleanse us of our destructive behaviors to self and others by His grace and mercy, however we may have to face some consequences from the choices we have made.

God's grace is one of His many beautiful no-strings-attached gifts He offers to all of us. We do nothing to earn it; it is free, totally and completely free! It is amazing that God is so good to us and loves us so much that he gives grace just for the asking. God's grace is abundant and everlasting. Holladay tells us that

> all of our lives are meant to be contained in His act of grace—what God has given us in and through Jesus Christ. Your forgiveness is contained in that act of grace. Your future is contained in that act of grace. Your relationships with God and with others are contained in God's great act of grace. (2008, p. 228)

The action of grace is essential as we talk about redemption. This includes a cleansing of our souls as we become ready to fully embrace God's love for us. If grace were not part of God's gift to us, then to be redeemed would take on another dimension, of which we would likely fail to achieve since we would be on our own. Jesus is our redeemer; He is the most evident example of God's grace for His people. God gave His son as the final sacrifice so all of us could be forgiven through grace as part of a new covenant with God's promises to His people. In Ephesians 1:6-8 we read:

> In Him we praise His glorious grace, which he has freely given us in the One he loves. In Him we have redemption through his blood, the forgiveness of sins, in accordance with the riches of God's grace. That He lavished on us with all wisdom and understanding.

To be cleansed from our past, all we have to do is reach out to Christ and believe in Him. Then ask for a clean heart and forgiveness for the unhealthy thoughts and actions we have lived. Because the definition of cleanse, according to the Life Application Bible, is "to make clean or pure", we know we need to seek strength and understanding in our desires to become new in the eyes of Christ.

The following Scriptures provide biblical support for the principle of cleansing:

- Wash away my iniquity and cleanse me from my sin. Psalm 51:2
- If a man cleanses himself from the latter, he will be an instrument for noble purposes, made holy useful to the Master and prepared to do any good work. 2 Timothy 2:21
- How much more, then, will the blood of Christ, who through the eternal Spirit offered Himself unblemished to God, cleanse our consciences from acts that lead to death, so that we may serve the living God? Hebrews 9:14
- Let us draw nearer to God with a sincere heart in full assurance of faith, having our hearts sprinkled to cleanse us from a guilty conscience and having our bodies washed with pure water. Hebrews 10:22
- "You are already clean because of the word I have spoken to you. Remain in me and I will remain in you." John 15:3

Discussion Points

A redemptive heart is something we need to continue to develop over time. Yes, God has forgiven our sins and we know that through His grace we are given His promise to be with us throughout our journey. What does that journey entail? Read through the questions to follow and create answers that explain your own journey and where you are in the process.

a. What does it mean to you to have a redemptive heart?

b. What can you do to continue your own redemption?

c. What is the most difficult barrier you experience for staying on track?

d. How will you know when your soul has been cleansed?

e. When was the last time you knew God extended grace to you?

f. When was the last time you provided grace to someone else?

Prayer

Thank You, Jesus, for the many times You have given us grace over and above that which we really deserved. Thank You for offering us a chance to cleanse our souls and develop a redemptive heart. Keep us on track, Lord, as we learn to live for You and keep our eyes on You as we make decisions that affect both our families and us. In Your name we pray, Amen.

Living by Example

> In everything set them an example by doing what is good. Titus 2:7

As noted in the Scripture above, we can determine that part of our cleansing, through redemption, is identified by how we present ourselves in our future work and relationships. Paul, as mentor and guide to Timothy, explained the importance of staying close to God in all things. Paul reminded Timothy that the world continues to present evil situations that can lead to moving away rather than closer to God. The importance of becoming the kind of person God can use for His own purposes requires staying close to the example of Christ's leading and focusing on being an instrument to others, by example, whenever God calls us to action. All of us can be God's messengers through our actions and words. As leaders, we become ambassadors for Christ and therefore it is important to find the right *fit* as you share God's Word with others. This is done by going to prayer and asking God to use you for His purpose. He will make it evident to you and He will reveal what He is calling you to do for His kingdom. Pastor Ron Faus explained that God's Kingdom is not a far off place but rather right here and now where we live, work, and play. We are responsible to provide evidence of the reign of God in His kingdom as based on what we do to represent Him. It is about what we do to spread the Word by showing the love of Christ through our actions (personal communication, June 9, 2013).

In John 15, Jesus teaches of the vine and the branches. This particular example of how Jesus works with us teaches of the importance of *bearing fruit* so that others will come to know Christ. Jesus explains that He is the vine and we are the branches and without Him we will wither and die. The story shows us that we are called to stay close to Him and bring others to understand His love for us. However, He also illustrates that we can claim to be a believer in Him but true followers are those who bring change among unbelievers. As part of His family of followers we are expected to share the good news of His love for His children. Interestingly, Jesus also talks about pruning of the branches. The Life Application Study Bible (2005) explains the two types of pruning of which Jesus speaks. The pruning may include a separation or a cutting back of the branches. The distinction refers to the possibility of needing to experience a *pruning* (discipline) so that we develop a stronger character and deeper faith. This illustrates to us that our lives are not to be free from facing the consequences of our actions and that God will use our difficulties to bring us closer to Him and to help us become better witnesses to His love and power. However, it is also noted that those who claim to follow Him and yet do nothing to enhance the growth of others (bearing fruit) will be considered useless and be *tossed aside* (separation) (p. 1775). As leaders and examples to others, it is our responsibility to help anyone who does not have a personal relationship with Christ come to Him and grow in commitment to His purpose. In John 15:3-4 we read:

> You are already clean because of the word I have spoken to you. Remain in me, and I will remain in you. No branch can bear fruit by itself; it must remain in the vine. Neither can you bear fruit unless you remain in me.

We discussed earlier that we all face the consequences of our actions, which may include some pruning as we learn to follow God's laws. However, the Scripture also tells us that this is a good thing because God is our Father and loves us, as a father is to love their child. Children are a blessing (Psalm 127:3) and are to be disciplined and shown the right way to live (Proverbs 6:20-23).

So, how do we accept the consequences of our actions when God builds our character by allowing us to live with the results of those actions? Galatians 6:7 reads:

> Do not be deceived. God cannot be mocked. A man reaps what he sows. The one who sows to please his sinful nature, from the nature will reap destruction; the one who sows to please the Spirit, from the Spirit will reap eternal life.

This Scripture reiterates that we must take responsibility for that which we cause to happen in our lives, and which ultimately leads to self-destruction or to hurting others. God will not intervene if you choose to hurt yourself in some way. He gives you a free will to do as you wish. However, if you choose to ask Him to help you change your habits or negative behaviors, He will do exactly that. Just remember, there are still consequences for the choices you have made; physical and emotional health problems, broken relationships, loss of a job or home, financial ruin, etc. Do you wish to continue down a road to ruin or to find God's voice and dedicate yourself to His plan for your life? The choice is yours.

Discussion Points

This section is a tough one because it provides truth in our behaviors that can cause us to feel very uncomfortable or even ashamed of the choices we have made over time. The good news is that your life does not have to remain in darkness. There is always light waiting on the other side of what has felt so out of control and impossible to change. Think about the following questions and respond honestly to each of them.

a. If God could write on your heart, what would you like Him to write?

b. What actions do you see in others who represent God's love through example?

c. What do you do to represent how God uses you as His messenger? Or do you?

d. What areas would you like to become more involved as God's instrument?

e. What areas need to be pruned in you so that you bear fruit in your life?

f. What consequences are you experiencing due to the choices you have made?

g. What can you do to remove the negatives in your life and move toward the light of God's love?

Prayer

We come to You today, Heavenly Father, seeking understanding about the behaviors we have chosen in our lives. Help us to understand how these behaviors hold us captive and prevent the personal freedom You offer us. Show us Your way and guide us through each day as we continue to strive to release the power of negativity and destruction that has led us to destructive choices. We take full responsibility for the decisions we have made in our lives that have caused broken relationships, harmful physical problems, and a tendency to avoid Your presence in our lives. We ask all of this in Jesus' name. Amen

Believe With all of Your Heart

> But when he asks, he must believe and not doubt, because he who doubts is like a wave of the sea, blown and tossed by the wind. James 1:6

Although we have mentioned the issue of doubt earlier in this book, it is necessary to look at it a bit deeper in this section. As we continue to learn about redemption and the cleansing of our sinful natures, an area that often surfaces is that of doubt. Sometimes the changes we need to make just seem so overwhelming and so terribly difficult that we have doubt in our own ability to have the necessary endurance to master the needed change. Our hearts tell us to stop doubting and believe that Christ is the answer and yet we live in a society whereby science is prevalent and important among scholars and political leaders. Technology has consumed our daily lives and the media places importance on data and tangible facts when looking at problem solving techniques. As Christ followers, faith is the pathway to understanding what God has called us to do. Living among those who fall to scientific principles can cause confusion and doubt in that which we cannot see for ourselves. At this point in the study, I would like to consider how fear, confusion, and definitely some doubt intertwine with what we hope to find through Christ. Not only is it hard to grasp that God will forgive us and cleanse us from the sins that have consumed us over time, we may find it difficult to internalize an all-knowing God who we cannot see. It is important to understand that this feeling is very normal and even expected among newer believers and seekers of the truth. Even people in the Bible had times of doubt and Jesus helped them understand those feelings and come to terms with how to remove the doubt through His leading.

It is always difficult to understand why pain and suffering must be a part of our lives and such events often cause us to doubt God's ways, especially if we have fallen victim to hurtful actions placed against our will. However, Meyer reminds us that we do not need to assume our future will be affected by our past (2005). Learning to rely on God in all things, having faith that He is in control, and trusting that His ways will be used to His purpose, which leads us to further growth and understanding, can be difficult and confusing. We are called to be open to the fears and doubts of others without criticism or judgment, even when it is hard to do. Heald wrote in her book <u>Becoming a Woman of Faith</u>:

> My greatest moments of doubt come when I question God's ways. Pain, suffering, and trials will always be in my life and in the lives of those I love. God challenges me to keep going into a land flowing with milk and honey, but there are still giants to contend with. In my "little" faith I doubt the goodness and faithfulness of the Lord. I believe that He is always with me, but when the winds begin to whip up the waves, I cry out for the Lord to wake me up. (2000, pp. 13-14)

Ultimately, we need to fully understand that no matter what is causing us to question our belief, no matter what the circumstance or how impossible it may seem, or who is involved in the situation, the only way to solve the problem is through going to Christ to support and guide us. He is the only one that can truly resolve the issue and our job will always be to believe in Him, with faith and assurance that He is with us. Christ is the answer to any problem, as long as we reach out in faith and trust, knowing He will provide the solution. It may mean waiting on His perfect timing or finding His answers are not what we had hoped for or anticipated. But, remember He knows our hearts (Luke 16:15) and He knows what will benefit us by knowing what we need (Philippians 4:19). By removing the doubt in His ability to lead, peace can overcome any situation and we will find comfort in Him. "When you are apprehensive about the troubles around you and doubt Christ's presence or ability to help, you must remember that He is the *only* one who can really help" (Living Application Bible, 2005, p. 1564).

The following Scriptures provide biblical support for the principle of doubt:

> Jesus replied, I tell you the truth, if you have faith and do not doubt, not only can you do what was done to the fig tree, but also you can say to this mountain, Go throw yourself into the sea, and it will be done. If you believe you will receive whatever you ask for in prayer. Matthew 21:21-22

Note: According to the Life Application Bible (NIV) (2005) notation, this Scripture is not suggesting that the disciples use faith as magic to actually move a mountain. Rather, Jesus is making a strong point about the lack of faith that His disciples were demonstrating at the time. It is important to note that when we pray, we should be less focused on our own interests and concentrate on that of what God may be planning for us. Pray that you are asking for God's will in the situation.

- Therefore I tell you, whatever you ask for in prayer, believe that you have received it, and it will be yours. Mark 11:24

- He said to them, why are you troubled, and why do doubts rise in your minds? Luke 24:38
- For my Father's will is that everyone who looks to the Son and believes in him shall have eternal life, and I will raise him up at the last day. John 6:40
- And without faith it is impossible to please God, because anyone who comes to him must believe that he exists and that he rewards those who earnestly seek him. Hebrews 11:6
- Be merciful to those who doubt. Jude 1:22

As you can see with the chosen Scriptures, much of the information is based on the doubt that the disciples of Christ experienced. If those who walked with Jesus felt times of doubt, is it any wonder that we who base all understanding on our faith, will experience times of doubt as well? Perhaps doubt can lead to growth as we search to understand more deeply what God is calling us to do.

Discussion Points

Doubt is not uncommon; it was something that we find happened even by those who worked closely with Christ. Remember, even Thomas would not believe Christ had returned after His death until he saw Jesus himself (John 20:27). As humans we also have times of doubt. When we fall short of meeting the expectations we have for ourselves and feel God is not reachable, we can fail to draw upon our faith and find ourselves falling into the depths of doubt.

a. When you think about your own faith, where are you experiencing doubts?

b. What areas in your life cause you to struggle with feeling God will be faithful to His promises?

c. How strong do you feel your own faith is at this time?

d. When you pray, do your prayers focus on your own interests or that of God's?

e. When does doubt seem to get in the way of your own growth in Christ?

Prayer

Thank You Heavenly Father for allowing us to grow in our faith through the trials of every day life. Help us to understand more fully Your power over our life and to trust You in all things. Remind us, Lord, that our prayer should reflect Your will and not our own desires so that we represent You to all who know us. Allow us to work on building a stronger faith and less times of doubt. In Your son's name we pray. Amen

Communicating With God in Prayer

If you believe, you will receive whatever you ask for in
prayer. Matthew 21:22

I want men everywhere to lift up holy hands in prayer,
without anger or disputing. 1 Timothy 2:8

Although there are many Scriptures available about prayer, these
particular verses, as explained in the Life Application Bible (NIV,
2005) are to show that God does expect us to pray in all things,
but prayer is also not something that is honored if it is not part
of God's will for us. He will not grant prayers that are harmful
to others or us; He will not honor a prayer that does not serve the
purpose of His plan for your life. "The stronger our belief, the
more likely our payers will be in line with God's will, and then
God will be happy to grant them" (p. 1579). Does this mean our
prayers will be answered immediately? Not always, remember
God has a perfect plan for our lives and He will provide the
answers we seek when the time is right even if the answer is not
what we had hoped for.

I find that all too often we expect God to answer our prayers
immediately and when He does not we feel He does not care or
is not really out there. There will be times when God responds in
unexpected ways and that His plan for us is always better than
what we can imagine for ourselves. Sometimes God blesses us with
an answer to a concern or question that was far more satisfying
than we ever dreamed we deserved. And, we may experience times
when a prayer was answered before we knew we needed to pray
in the first place. The point is God's plan is the perfect plan even
though it may mean waiting on Him in His perfect timing.

As we pray we must also understand the importance of having faith that God will answer and deliver that which He knows to be in our best interest and to that which follows His purpose. Storms, as cited in Heald, 2000, wrote:

> Believing that we shall receive it will not force God to do something he otherwise opposes . . . Faith enough to meet the condition for such a prayer to be answered would have to come from God. When God wishes to grant a request on condition of wholehearted beliefs, he himself produces that belief in the heart of His child. (p. 68)

Storms is explaining the importance of faith in prayer with the understanding that God will provide the desire in our hearts to pray and believe that He will answer in a way that is best for us. Billy Graham often preached on faith and wrote several books that included faith as a principle element of prayer. He stated:

> Faith is rationally impossible where there is nothing to believe. Faith must have an object. The object of Christian faith is Christ. Faith means more than an intellectual assent to the claims of Christ. Faith involves the will. It is volitional. Faith demands action. If we actually believe, then we will live. Faith without works is dead. Faith actually means surrender and commitment to the claims of Christ. (1984, p. 181)

One fallacy that we can put aside regarding prayer is that we need to have just the right words when we petition God through prayer. Nowhere in the Bible does it say to be formal in how we speak to God; Just the opposite. Jesus warns us when he said, "And when you pray, do not keep on babbling like pagans, for they think they will be heard because of their many words. Do not be like them, for your Father knows what you need before you ask him." Jesus is telling us that prayer is very personal and between you and God. There may even be times when you do not know how to pray. I have experienced this in times of fear and stress. At those times I just say, *Jesus help me, you know what is needed.* A prayer is not a method used to convince God you are in need, it is just your heart speaking to Him in love and faith, knowing that He will be there for you.

Discussion Points

Think about the following questions while reflecting on your life as a woman of God. Decide how the questions relate specifically to you and where you are at this time in your journey.

a. When have you experienced a time that prayer did not seem to work?

b. Share a time when you prayed for something but God did not answer immediately or He answered in an unexpected way.

c. When do you feel you are most likely to hear God's *voice?*

d. What is the most difficult thing for you regarding prayer?

e. When you pray, what do you typically talk about with God?

f. How well would you say your prayer life and your faith that God will answer are connected?

Prayer

Our dear Heavenly Father, we thank You for being so faithful in Your Word and in the promises You have given to us. We know You are waiting for us to come to You with any and all of our concerns and desires. We thank You for the opportunity to pray to You and to know You are always just a prayer away. Help us to be faithful to our prayer life and to remember that You want only what is best for us. Please forgive us for all we have done that has not been pleasing to You. In Jesus' name, Amen

Praising God in Prayer

> I will extol the Lord at all times; his praise will always be on my lips. Psalm 34:1

Most of what we have addressed with prayer has included asking or requesting something from God. We have noted the importance of prayer with faith and growing to understand that God will not answer all prayers, at least in the way we expect. An important element of prayer that is often overlooked is that of praising God with a thankful heart. The definition of praise, according to the Life Application Bible (NIV, 2005) is "to worship, commend, or to give honor to" (p. 2355). Therefore we honor God by finding joy in what He does for us: For that we should be grateful and praise Him. Generally, we are so caught up in our daily lives that we forget to be thankful for the blessings that we receive each day. Voskamp (2010) studied the term Eucharisteo and its meaning in Greek. She found it was used at the time Christ was giving thanks at the Last Supper and in her study she found the word reflects three specific terms: thanksgiving, grace, joy. She continues to challenge us to think about how being thankful leads to grace and joy. Thus, when Christ said "Be joyful always; pray continually; give thanks in all circumstances, for this is God's will for you in Christ Jesus" (1 Thessalonians 5:16), He was depicting how we are to respond to what God does for us in every situation of our lives.

In the book of Psalms, David showed much rejoicing when he was reconciled with God after times of disobedience. The Scripture found in Psalm 92:1-2 states, "It is good to praise the Lord and make music to your name, O Most High, to proclaim your love in the morning and your faithfulness at night." David was showing full gratitude of what God had done for him and by having a thankful heart and praising God's name, David became a model of goodness as found through God's love for His people. Dr. David Jeremiah reminds us that with the spirit of God in us we can overcome negativity and begin to notice those things in life to be thankful for rather than being someone who finds constant fault or who spends a great deal of time complaining. Our gratitude to God and our ability to praise Him for the blessings He provides, puts us in a place of joy and thanksgiving. "He will give us victory over those negative, self-pitying thoughts" (1998, p. 207). How then do we praise God for what He has done for us? How often do we remember to talk to Him each day? Where do we find the time to ensure we are spending time with God to praise Him and thank Him? Dr. Billy Graham suggests we pray continually throughout the day and to make the action of prayer a common activity that becomes second nature to what we do throughout our busy lives (1984). The challenge for all of us is to be in a spirit of prayer and thanksgiving regardless of where we are or what we are doing.

Discussion Points

Using this section as a reminder to pray at all times about everything, think about how such a commitment will work into your own life. How will you praise God in times of difficulty? Use the scenarios below and think about how you would pray if you experienced these events.

Scenario #1: Company is coming for dinner and you are on a very limited budget with nothing in the freezer to offer. Your mom gave you a roast so you decided to use your crock-pot to cook it with potatoes and carrots. You went to work with a plan to have a nice evening with your friends. You got home from work one hour before the company was to arrive and were ready to fix a salad to go with the roast. As you entered the house you realized you did not smell the aroma you had planned on. Rather, you smelled an electric odor that seemed to flow throughout the entire house. The crock-pot was broken!

Prayer:

Scenario #2: Your daughter is home from school with a fever. You have her settled in with tissues, aspirin, and a cup of chicken soup simmering on the stove. She begins vomiting and you run to her aide, dropping the cup of soup and tripping over the dog. You fell down and twisted your ankle.

Prayer:

Scenario #3: You are late for a job interview and realize this may be your last chance for a while to get a job. Your car is fairly reliable but you have been very low on money and just as you got into the car you realize the gas tank is sitting on empty.

Prayer:

Now that you have practiced thinking about the above situations and how to pray, think of one time in your life where a situation had you in a panic about what to do. What was the situation and how did you handle it? If you had to go through it again, what would your prayer be?

Prayer

Oh, dear Lord in Heaven, it is so hard to have a spirit of praise in all things. Life can be so challenging and difficult in so many ways. When things seem to pile up and a solution feels very far away, our spirit is tired and often confused. We are so thankful that You are always just a breath away and we know in our hearts You can solve all of our problems if we just trust You to do so. Help us to learn how to be grateful for everything in life, even those things that are impossible to understand. Show us Your love and patience as we continue to find the way through difficulty. Thank You, Lord, for always loving us. In Your name we pray, Amen

Conclusion

Facing redemption can be difficult and painful for most people who are struggling to feel God's grace in their lives. To be fully redeemed, it is necessary to allow God to be your one and only answer to the problems you experience, no matter how big or how small. The challenge in this chapter is to understand God's presence and communication through prayer. It is necessary that we all learn more about faith and how to rely on God when we face times of spiritual isolation. As women grow closer to God they will experience a desire and need for spiritual cleansing and renewal through the redemption process. Part of the action will be found within the ability to help them live their lives, as Christ would call them to live, while honoring Him through becoming like Him. Prayer and belief in what Christ can do is instrumental in the redemption process so that women will learn to humbly come to Him at all times. It is worthy to understand that redemption is a process and not necessarily a *quick fix* for anyone who has led a life of poor choices and harmful habits. It will take some women longer than others to grasp the concept of redemption and to feel completely worthy of God's love.

CHAPTER 7

Humbling Self:
Reconciliation

> Leave your gift at the altar and there remember
> that your brother has something against you, leave
> your gift there in front of the altar. First go and be
> reconciled to your brother; then come and offer your
> gift. Matthew 5:23-24

I n this Scripture Jesus addresses an issue of claiming love for
God while having a hostile heart against someone else. From
this understanding comes the realization that we cannot
have it both ways; we cannot hate anyone and still maintain we
love the creator (God). Jesus is calling us to make things right,
through reconciliation, with those you are in conflict with then,
and only then, you are pure of heart and able to honestly assert
your love for God. The Living Application Study Bible (2005)
explains:

> Broken relationships can hinder our relationship with
> God. If we have a problem or grievance with a friend,
> we should resolve the problem as soon as possible.
> We are hypocrites if we claim to love God while we

hate others. Our attitudes toward others reflect our relationship with God. (1 John 4:20)

We will use the following definition of reconciliation for the purpose of this study: "To restore harmony between persons, especially between God and human beings" (Life Application Study Bible, NIV, 2005, p. 2358). This definition would include the concept of healing broken relationships between each other and with God whether due to circumstances of your own doing or that of situations beyond your control. An example being, a child who was molested by an adult may find it impossible to have a relationship with the abuser and yet God calls us to remove the bitter feelings we may have and the anger it produces and forgive, as we have been forgiven (Ephesians 4:31-32) and to love and pray for our enemies (Matthew 5:44). Reconciling the relationship may feel impossible for the victim of abuse and yet we are called to put the offense aside so as not to destroy who we are or our relationship with Christ. We are not commanded however to maintain an ongoing relationship with the abuser.

Judging Others

Do not judge, and you will not be judged. Do not condemn, and you will not be condemned. Forgive, and you will be forgiven. Give, and it will be given to you. A good measure, pressed down, shaken together and running over, will be poured into your lap. For with the measure you use, it will be measured to you. Luke 6:37-38

We love because he first loved us. If anyone says, "I love God," yet hates his brother, he is a liar. For

> anyone who does not love his brother, whom he has
> seen, cannot love God, whom he had not seen. And
> he has given us this command: Whoever loves God
> must also love his brother. I John 4:19-21

As stated before, God has created us to be relational and it is relevant to consider that our attitudes toward others reflect how we think about and relate to God. After all, we are created in His image (Genesis 1:27). He wants first and foremost for us to be in relationship with Him and as presented in the Ten Commandments we are to honor Him in all things by putting none other before Him (Deuteronomy 5:7). He has called us to be His servant and to worship Him through honor and praise. God will forgive us for our weaknesses and our sin. He will allow us to restore a relationship with Him through repentance, forgiveness, and redemption. But, what does this mean for the relationships destroyed among our family and friends while we were not following God's plan? In order to restore relationships it may mean we will need to humble ourselves to those of which we are in conflict. It also may mean to put aside that which was done to us by someone else. It does not mean we must forget what happened or to spend our days with the offender, it just means to clear our hearts and minds of the ugliness that was not our doing in the first place. This clearing can only happen by forgiving the person, even though we are not forgiving the action.

To be reconciled means to cast off those things in your life that causes you to draw away from those who may have hurt you or have disappointed you in the past. Put God first in all things and look to Him to give you strength and courage to address the difficult task of forgiveness and reconciliation. This means it is necessary to but Christ first, before family, career, position, etc. (Pastor Griswold, personal communication, October 14, 2012). Understanding and becoming part of God's Kingdom requires action and perseverance when Jesus calls us to His purpose, which means to place Him as the priority in your life. As you come to reconcile with your differences between your family, friends, and even with yourself, Jesus is the only pathway to a successful conclusion. It is not up to you to find fault and give judgment for how others have treated you. Judging the actions of others belongs only to God, "There is only one Lawgiver and Judge, the one who is able to save and destroy. But you—who are you to judge your neighbor?" (James 4:12).

Discussion Points

As an activity in learning to turn away from making judgments, this activity will allow you to privately practice nonjudgmental behaviors that Christ teaches us to use with those of whom we are in conflict. Write on a piece of paper the name of a person who is part of a broken relationship with you and one of whom you feel a need to grow toward reconciliation. I will not ask you to reveal the name but I do ask you to pray silently for that person while holding the paper in your hand.

Following the silent prayer, discuss the following:

> a. Why it is difficult to pray for that person?
>
> b. State one word that describes your feelings at the moment.

c. Why is this activity so difficult? Or is it?

d. Do you feel like you are judging the person or their actions?

e. How would you want someone you hurt to judge you?

f. What can you do to begin the process of reconciliation?

Leader notes: This can be a very difficult exercise for some women who have had years of abuse or life controlling issues that are not yet ready to be resolved. Have patience with each person as they face some very difficult memories. Do not push too hard, keep the door open for future conversations on an individual basis if needed.

Prayer

Heavenly Father we come to You at this time with an open heart and willing desire to find the path to reconciliation with those we have hurt in the past and who have hurt us. We ask for a repentant heart of understanding and the strength to recognize our sins as we openly admit to You where we have failed. Lord please help us to recognize our sinful nature so that we may fully reveal to You the sins we have committed. Help us to have the faith we need to move toward You knowing You will hold our hand as we face the difficulty of reconciling with our families and friends in a way that allows us to be a shining example of Your love. Show us Your desires in all things giving us strength to continue when things become difficult. In Your son's name, Amen.

Reconciling with God and Others

If anyone says, "I love God," yet hates his brother, he is a liar. For anyone who does not love his brother, whom he has seen, cannot love God, whom he has not seen. And he has given us this command: Whoever loves God must also love his brother. John 4:20-21

Since reconciliation means restoring harmony, it appears that some specific work will need to be done to restore broken relationships that have caused any kind of emotional division. Would it not be easier to ignore the situation or the person? Probably, at least for a while: However, if the person in question is part of your family, it is likely you cannot ignore them, not forever any way. God placed us in the families we have for a reason, not a reason to be hurt but to be relational. Sin happens in our lives, sometimes to us and sometimes by us, but it does happen. That sin can then lead to destructive behaviors that ruin families. We have discussed a great deal about forgiveness earlier in this book and the next step is reconciling with the people you have forgiven or who have forgiven you. I am not saying it is easy, on the contrary it is very difficult and takes humility and inner strength. All you can do is try. If the person does not want to reconcile, you cannot force it, but you must free yourself from the ugliness of the trouble between you. This can only happen if you make the effort to do your part. Reconciliation will not happen, though, until you have honestly forgiven the person in question. Remember, you are not condoning what was done and you are not accepting the blame all on yourself, if it is not your doing. You are not agreeing to live your life around them continually and you are not pretending the infraction never happened. However, you are showing compassion and a willingness to free yourself from the stress and pain of separation.

Although it would be nice to reconcile with those of which you have been in conflict, it is not realistic to think it will happen in all cases. Reconciliation takes two people and even if you have forgiven them, they may not want to reconcile at all. There will be some things that happen in your relationships that just can never be the same and therefore reconciliation may not happen (Kendall, 2002). However, to be free of any psychological or physiological effects, it may at least be necessary to attempt to work through the relationship. When feelings are subjected to signs of unresolved anger, we need to go to God with the issue because He commands us to put away our anger (Ephesians 4:26). Meyer (2005) wrote, "A wounded person cannot receive emotional healing while remaining angry" (p. 144). Reconciliation cannot be forced on either side of the issue, but should be prayed about asking God for understanding of how to handle the situation, especially if it is causing emotional or physical damage. Professional help may be an option in some cases whereby the memories have been repressed or negative symptoms are evident. God does not tell us we cannot be angry, but He does say we should not sin in the process (Ephesians 4:26).

Discussion Points

Reconciliation can be difficult and a slow process. When we are able to forgive or be forgiven it is the first step to reaching reconciliation. As stated above, not all relationships can be reconciled, but an effort to do so will help relieve the stress of unresolved issues with those you care about. Answer and discuss the following questions as you think about those of whom you may wish to receive reconciliation.

a. Who are those who you feel may not be ready for reconciliation from a broken relationship with you? Who do you think you may be able to begin the process of reconciliation?

b. List the areas of greatest fear that causes you to hesitate to reconcile with someone.

e. What responsibilities do you have to bring about reconciliation?

f. Where might you find support for building a broken relationship?

g. What steps can you take to begin the process of reconciling with those who have hurt you and those you have hurt?

God Pursues His Children

> For the Son of Man came to seek and to save what
> was lost. Luke 19:10

God never stops pursuing us. He wants us to be with Him for eternity and is always waiting for us to make the decision to be His completely. It is our job to watch, listen, and accept His invitation. The parable of the Prodigal Son is my favorite parable told by Jesus and an excellent illustration of the principle of God pursuing His children. As explained in Luke 15:20-24, this parable shows us that as with the father in the story, God will not hold us against our will if we desire to move away from Him. He will let us go but He will never stop looking for us to return. God will welcome us back no matter what and will not place guilt upon our hearts when we return to Him. This is the true essence of reconciliation as God demonstrates, no matter how much or what we have done, He will forgive, love, and accept us back to Him. Pastor Hal Schrader shared that God will meet us where we are unclean. He does not wait for us to "clean up" before He agrees to take us back, but rather, God will do the work of cleaning us up. As we turn to Him for forgiveness, he then removes our disgrace (personal communication, March 10, 2013). Note that "before you were a believer, God sought you; and he is still seeking those who are yet lost" (Life Application Bible, NIV, 2005, p. 1707).

As God continues to pursue each of us, He wants to help us reach the *light* of His kingdom, the light that is He and He alone. God helps us to walk in the light and remove ourselves from darkness; we can then be assured that we are on the right path when we use God's Word as our guide. Moore, in her book <u>Get Out of</u>

That Pit: Straight Talk about God's Deliverance, wrote, "God chases you down with melody and hems you in with harmony until your raptured soul finds liberty and your aching feet find stability" (2007, p. 195). To better grasp an understanding of pursuit, it will be helpful to read and study the Bible so that we may fully embrace God's plan in His pursuit to draw us back to Him. Note that it is perfectly OK to find the version of the Bible that is easiest for you to understand. I do suggest the use of a Study Bible when possible so as to have more clarification provided when looking for the answers with helpful explanation. The Bible is the best possible road map for believers to use when trying to figure out how we all fit in the world and how we can best please God. The Bible is truly the light that ensures our safety as we walk through the trials and dangers of life. The Life Application Bible states:

> To walk safely in the woods at night we need a light so we don't trip over tree roots or fall into holes. In this life we walk through a dark forest of evil. But the Bible can be our light to show us the way ahead so we won't stumble as we walk. It reveals the entangling roots of false values and philosophies. Study the Bible so you will be able to see your way clear enough to stay on the right path. (NIV, 2005, p. 958)

Consider that God is the light of your life. He is representative of what is good in the world, reliable, truthful, pure, and holy. Your goal should be to live in the light, the light that is Jesus Christ. Avoid the darkness of evil, which leads to sin and destruction. Allow Christ to enter within your spirit and welcome Him as the author of your life. Continue to pursue Him as he pursues you.

Discussion Points

At this point take time to read and discuss the following two parables about God pursuing us to reconcile with Him; The Parable of the Lost Sheep (Luke 15:3-7) and the Parable of the Lost Coin (Luke 15:8-10) as an addition to the Parable of the Lost Son (The Prodigal Son, Luke 15: 11-31). Read the parables in the group and discuss the meaning behind the words of Jesus.

Parable of the Lost Sheep:

Suppose one of you has a hundred sheep and loses one of them. Does he not leave the ninety-nine in the open country and go after the lost sheep until he finds it? And when he finds it, he joyfully puts it on his shoulders and goes home. Then he calls his friends and neighbors together and says, 'Rejoice with me; I have found my lost sheep.' I tell you that in the same way there will be more rejoicing in heaven over one sinner who repents than over ninety-nine righteous persons who do not need to repent.

Parable of the Lost Coin:

Or suppose a woman has ten silver coins and loses one. Does she not light a lamp, sweep the house ad search carefully until she finds it? And when she finds it, she calls her friends and neighbors together and says, 'Rejoice with me; I have found my lost coin.' In the same way, I tell you, there is rejoicing in the presence of the angels of God over one sinner who repents.

a. Which of the three parables can you identify with most and why?

b. Who in your own life do you feel would treat you as the father did his son in the story of the Prodigal Son?

c. Are you running away from God or to God?

d. When do you feel most loved and supported?

e. What can you do to improve your feeling of acceptance by God?

f. There will always be times when we do not feel as close to God as at other times. When do you find yourself most likely to feel distance between you and God? What can you do to draw closer to Him?

Because we understand the feeling of darkness when we are without God in our lives, it is important to focus on moving toward the light. Christ is the light of the world and we are in the world facing it either with Him or without Him. It is ultimately our own choice as to how we choose to function. As with the Parables above, we know God rejoices each time a lost person comes back to Him and chooses to live a life as divinely designed by our creator. Finding the light is up to us, we are called to remove ourselves from the darkness (Satan) and live for the light (Christ).

When we find ourselves falling away from God and being tempted to return to bad habits that have proven to be dangerous or unhealthy, it is time to remember that those who lived under the rule of Satan for so long will likely experience moments of weakness. Satan does not give up on us once he has had us under his control. I often explain this idea to the women I work with as similar to a jealous boyfriend. He has had your undivided attention, your loyalty, and your devotion. He likes the idea of being worshipped by you and your willingness to try to please Him. Once you have decided the relationship is over, he becomes more diligent and attentive trying to win you back. He will tempt you with the things he knows you have come to enjoy and he will remind you over and over of the good times you have had together. He will lie to you and destroy other relationships so as to have you all to himself. It is not a great deal different than the angry boyfriend who stalks you and waits until you are vulnerable and weak and then makes his move to win you back. Satan's pursuit is for evil purposes, he wants to control you and cause havoc in your life. He is the darkness and only Christ can distinguish his fire. Christ wants to show you how His power can remove your sin and give you peace. His desire is to help you find healing and healthy relationships as you walk in His light.

Discussion Points

Read each of the following Scriptures regarding walking in the light and discuss the questions that follow.

- You, O Lord, keep my lamp burning; my God turns my darkness into light. Psalm 18:28
- Blessed are those who have learned to acclaim you, who walk in the light of your presence, O Lord. Psalm 89:15
- Your Word is a lamp to my feet and a light for my path. Psalm 119:105
- Come, O house of Jacob, let us walk in the light of the Lord. Isaiah 2:5

a. Which of the Scriptures speak most personally to you? Why?

b. Describe how Christ is a light to you.

c. When do you need to call on the light of the Lord the most?

d. When are you a light to another person?

e. What can you do to develop a stronger inclination to turn from the darkness and to walk into the light?

f. How does walking in the light relate to reconciliation, as you understand it?

Prayer

Thank You, Lord, for always pursuing us and never giving up. We thank You and praise you for the opportunities to feel whole and healthier as we learn more about You and Your plan for our lives. Your voice is becoming clearer and we are beginning to feel closer to You in our walk. The journey is long but the experiences are building our desire to know more about how to follow You. Thank you for showing us how to walk in the light and for being that light in our dark world. In Your name we pray, Amen.

Road to Salvation

> Restore to me the joy of your salvation and grant me
> a willing sprit, to sustain me. Psalm 51:12

As we continue to look at reconciliation and have had time to discuss the need to reconcile with friends or family, the next steps are to discuss reconciliation with God. In Romans, the tenth chapter we read about how God gives us an opportunity to receive the gift of salvation, which is a form of reconciliation with Him. Salvation cannot be earned but can be received without effort other than to have faith in God's purpose for His people. All we have to do is declare with our mouths and believe in our hearts that Christ died on the cross for us and then arose from the dead to become the living sacrifice (Life Application Study Bible, NIV, 2005, p. 1899). This process opens us up to reconciliation with Christ; to understand His plan and prosper as we become wholly and holy healed.

We are often reminded that we cannot lose our Salvation, and this is very true. Christ died for us so that we have the assurance of coming to God with humble hearts while expressing a desire to be saved my Him, so that we will one day be part of His heavenly kingdom. "Jesus gently but relentlessly asked people to make a decision about their relationship with him. The fundamental decision involved this invitation: Follow me. Come be with me and learn from me how to be like me" (Ortberg, 2005, p. 50). That same offer is given to us today. We are already a part of His earthly kingdom, but how we fit into His plan is dependant upon what we do each day as followers of Christ. The Life Application Bible (2005) defines salvation as, "deliverance from danger or difficulty; deliverance from the power or penalty of sin" (p. 2361). What the definition is telling us is that Jesus Christ died to represent the sins of man, present and future. Because He died for all of us, we now have an opportunity to speak to God through Jesus and ask for forgiveness when we fail, and we all fail from time to time because none of us live a life of perfection. As we continue to understand how Jesus died for us so that we may go to the Father through Jesus (John 14:6), we should remember that Satan does not go away. Instead he *beefs up* his action and power to persuade us to return to Him. Terkeurst wrote,

> Satan will do everything he can to convince you to say no to God. Satan's very name means "one who separates." He wants to separate you from God's best by offering what seems "very good" from a worldly perspective. He wants you to deny Christ's power in you. He wants to distract you from God's radical purpose for you. (2007, p. 61)

The process of being saved through faith results in your salvation and you will begin to see and feel a difference in yourself. In all likelihood you will not have an immediate epitome of understanding, especially if you have been away from God for a long period of time or have lost your belief in His presence in your life. Instead, you will begin to want to know more about how Jesus can be an active part of your life. You will want to be more involved with positive things and people in your life. You are evolving and coming closer to hearing God's voice and understanding your purpose. Dr. Billy Graham tells us that belief, through faith, is necessary if you are to receive salvation and become a new person in Christ (1984). But, remember, you cannot earn your salvation; it is God's gift to you by His grace. All you have to do is to believe that Jesus is your Savior and that He died for you and rose again. The Bible describes this as being born again and explains that we must be born again to enter into the Kingdom of God (John 3:7). The term *Born Again* simply means you are throwing out the old person you have been and becoming a new person through Christ Jesus. You are *born again* because you are a new being who now does not live by worldly standards but rather by what God is calling you to do in living for Him. In Graham's book <u>Peace with God</u>, he wrote:

No matter how soiled your past, no matter how snarled your present, no matter how hopeless your future seems to be—there is a way out. There is a sure, safe, everlasting way out—but there is only one! You have only one choice to make. You have only one path to follow, other than the torturous, unrewarding path you've been treading.

You can go on being miserable, discontented, frightened, unhappy, and disgusted with yourself and your life; or you can decide right now that you want to be born again. You can decide right now to wipe out your sinful past and make a new start, a fresh start, a right start. You can decide now to become the person that Jesus promised you could be. (1984, p. 166)

In addition to the regeneration of your new self, it should be noted that you cannot inherit Christianity or your salvation. Your Christian parents cannot pass salvation on through your genes and it is not part of your DNA. Just because you have gone to church since childhood does not automatically save you for God's kingdom. You must make a conscience decision to be born again through repentance of sin and a turning to Jesus through faith. Graham explains that

it is the infusion of divine life into the human soul. It is the implantation or importation of divine nature into the human soul whereby we become the children of God. We receive the breath of God. Christ through the Holy Spirit takes up residence in our hearts. We are attached to God for eternity. That means that if you have been born again you will live as long as

God lives, because you are now sharing His very life.
(pp. 170-171)

The following Scriptures provide biblical support for the principle of salvation. Although these do not include all Scriptures available, they provide good context for this important topic and to help participants obtain a deeper understanding:

- The Lord is my strength and my song; he has become my salvation. He is my God, and I will praise him, my father's God, and I will exalt him. Exodus 15:2
- But I trust in your unfailing love; my heart rejoices in your salvation. Psalm 13:5
- The Lord is my light and my salvation—whom shall I fear? The Lord is the stronghold of my life—who shall I be afraid? Psalm 27:1
- Restore to me the joy of your salvation and grant me a willing spirit, to sustain me. Psalm 51:12
- He alone is my rock and my salvation; he is my fortress. I will never be shaken. Psalm 62:2
- I am in pain and distress; may your salvation, O God, protect me. Psalm 69:29
- In the time of my favor I will answer you, and in the day of salvation I will help you. Isaiah 49:8a
- Salvation is found in no one else, for there is no other name under heaven given to men by which we must be saved. Acts 4:12
- I am not ashamed of the gospel, because it is the power of God for the salvation of everyone who believes. Romans 1:16a
- Godly sorrow brings repentance that leads to salvation and leaves no regret, but worldly sorrow brings death. 2 Corinthians 7:10

<u>Leader Notes:</u> The differences between the use of the word salvation in the old and new testaments may need some distinction dependant upon the biblical maturity of the participants. You may wish to discuss the principle of God incarnate in the man of Jesus Christ to develop a deeper understanding of salvation. If anyone in the group wishes to make a profession of faith and ask to be saved, you will want to provide that opportunity or have them meet with your pastor. I always encourage my ladies that after they accept Christ as their Savior, that it should be shared with others who love them.

Discussion Points

As you think about our discussion of salvation, respond to the following questions as they relate to your own personal understanding.

a. What might be going on in your life that prevents you from reconciling with God?

b. What other "gods" in your life impedes full reconciliation with God?

c. What does *born again* mean to you? Write your own definition.

Read the following Scriptures that were presented above and explain what they mean to you. They are repeated here for convenience and easy access in your study.

> a. I am in pain and distress; may your salvation, O God, protect me. Psalm 69:29
>
> b. Salvation is found in no one else, for there is no other name under heaven given to men by which we must be saved. Acts 4:12
>
> c. Godly sorrow brings repentance that leads to salvation and leaves no regret, but worldly sorrow brings death. 2 Corinthians 7:10

Prayer

Our dear Heavenly Father, thank You for the gift of salvation through Your son Jesus Christ. We understand the gift of salvation is free to us and that it cannot be earned but rather given freely so that we may reconcile fully with Your gift of love and relationship. Help us to realize the importance of freeing ourselves from hatred of others due to situations not designed by You. Open our hearts as Your presence is revealed through the healing of relationships. Thank you for helping us learn to live in a way where we may respond to Your will for us in how we live for You. Forgive us where we have failed You. In Jesus' name, Amen.

Conclusion

Reconciliation with God means to give up the old and accept the new. It is about change and taking the promises God gives to us for full forgiveness and understanding of God's plan for our lives including a part of us that is no longer the same. To be reconciled is to be changed. The change may be within us so that we may reconcile with God and use the relationship to grow in His purpose and plan for our lives. Reconciliation may refer to coming back together from a broken relationship whereby healing and forgiveness is needed. Sometimes we are the ones who need to be forgiven and at other times we need to do the forgiving of someone who has hurt us physically or emotionally. Reconciliation will not happen successfully without walking with God in the process. He is faithful to His promises that He will watch over us and walk with us in all times of fear and confusion. He does not give up on us and continually pursues us throughout our lives. It is up to us to also pursue God as the author of our hearts and the creator of our lives through His perfect plan. To gain peace within our hearts and souls it will require living for Christ and modeling our lives after Him. Reconciling with God may lead to a confession of faith that ultimately leads to our salvation whereby we are *born again* as new people devoted to God the Father. God wants his children to join Him in heaven one day and He is always ready to show us how to live for His kingdom through reconciliation.

CHAPTER 8

Freedom From Self Destruction: *Recovery*

Restore us to yourself, O lord, that we may return;
renew our days as of old. Lamentations 5: 21

And the God of all grace, who called you to his eternal
glory in Christ, after you have suffered a little while,
will himself restore you and make you strong, firm
and steadfast. I Peter 5:10

Recovery involves restoration and renewal as we discover
God's grace and mercy in our lives. It is about stopping
the cycle of self-destruction and moving toward newness
in spiritual, physical, and emotional well-being. As we discussed
in Chapter 6 and read in the Psalms we learn a great deal about
the life of David and his struggle to find his way back to God and
to be spiritually purified. In the story of David's infidelity with
Bathsheba he came to the realization that he needed to be cleansed
from within (51:7). "We must ask God to cleanse us from within,
clearing our hearts and spirits for new thoughts and desires.
Right conduct can come only from a clean heart and spirit" (Life
Application Study Bible, NIV, 2005, p. 881). Additionally, it is

important to look to God for the means to sustain the ability to work toward renewal. This will include surrounding yourself with those who can support your decision to be a part of God's kingdom. Find a community of people who will help sustain you as you wait on God to show you the way. He will make everything clear to you in His time and when you are ready to hear Him.

An area of difficulty that may interfere with full recovery is that of waiting on God. It is not uncommon for us to feel we are not hearing His voice; we struggle to know what to do and how to do it. Waiting on God is not unlike waiting for anything else we need or want badly. It seems to take forever, but to wait on God to show us the way will build inner strength and dedication to the process. What do you do when you do not hear His voice or fully understand His message to you? This experience is not uncommon and many of us face this dilemma at different times in our lives. When things are not clear and you are unsure about what God wants from you, just wait and trust. Is it easy to do that? No, it is not easy. But as you wait, God will use the time to work on you in a very specific way. He will help you become ready to receive His Word and do His work. The more you are rooted in the Word and surround yourself with supportive Bible-believing people, the easier it is for God to reach you and speak to your heart about what He is asking you to do. The Life Application Bible tells us "Hoping in the Lord is expecting that his promise of strength will help us to rise above life's distractions and difficulties" (2005, NIV, p. 1141).

Discussion Points

At this point in the study, you will see that strength is a key word for finding your place in God's plan. God loves all of us and does not limit His time to only those who seem to have the faith and understanding of how to follow Him. As we learned in the previous chapter, God pursues His children and that means all of us. Note that your responsibility is to stay with it until you are sure you know exactly what God is calling you to do. It may be something as simple as to work on your faith, read your Bible, or ask a mature Christian to mentor you. But it also means to remove Satan from your life. Honestly reflect on the following questions as you think about your future.

a. Where do you find your strength to develop a means to sustain your recovery?

b. Where are you in the process for your renewal?

c. Looking at from where you have come to where you hope to go, how to you hope to sustain the success of your plan?

d. What do you do to incorporate spiritual, physical, and emotional well-being?

e. What do you do to seek Him as you wait on the Lord?

Prayer

Thank You, Jesus, for always being with us in our time of need and in our time of celebration. We thank You for opening Your arms to us at all times and embracing us as Your children. We know You have not given up on us and we thank You for second chances and new beginnings. We need strength as we continue to look at how to be spiritually, physically, and emotionally healthy. Show us the way so that we are able to recognize what we need to do so that we are obedient to Your Word. We thank You for the many blessings You have graced us with. We love You and honor You. In Jesus' name we pray, Amen.

A Clear Conscience

> Against You, You only, have I sinned, and done this evil in Your sight. Psalm 51:4

> Wash me thoroughly from my iniquity, and cleanse me from my sin. Psalm 51:2

> My brothers, I have fulfilled my duty to God in all good conscience to this day. Acts 23:1

As we discussed earlier in Chapter 5 we know that guilt and shame can cause us to feel badly about choices we have made including those that have been self-destructive or hurtful to other people. We learned that emotions play a large part in how we develop or keep healthy relationships. The negative things we carry within ourselves can cause both physical and emotional damage and is something that must be addressed as we work toward full recovery. Dr. Jeremiah (2001) described guilt as "a giant with interesting powers . . . It kills slowly but with excruciating pain" (p. 73). Guilt leads to a need to clear your conscience so that the guilt felt from the sin committed can be cleansed from your soul and you can move on to face the world with peace in your heart. As explained in Psalm 32, this is exactly what David had to do. David lost his will to communicate with God and became consumed with debilitating silence, followed by deep sorrow. As David continued to struggle with his guilt he ultimately fell into a life of great secrecy, leading to isolation from friends and family. God sent an accuser to David, which helped him to realize that he must confess the sin by admitting his guilt to God and to begin the process of rebuilding relationships. "Confession is all about naked honesty before God or before fellow Christians. It means describing our actions with the same words God uses, and no dissembling or distortions" (Jeremiah, p. 79). Dr. Jeremiah is telling us that we cannot hide our sin from God and must not place the blame on others. We cannot be honest and still use words like; I was born this way, my parents caused me to do this, I was abused as a kid so it isn't my fault entirely, I was forced, etc. Instead, be honest about your part in the sin and you will develop an inner peace you have not felt in a long time.

Consider the purpose of clearing your conscience as a means to restore the joy that God wants for you. He did not create you to be unhappy, unhealthy, or unproductive. Dr. Jeremiah, in his book <u>Slaying the Giants in Your Life</u> (2001) wrote:

> We can't lose our salvation, but we can certainly lose
> some of the fringe benefits. Some of us do things that
> displease God, and we never face up to them. The

time comes when we realize our lives are grim and joyless. (p. 82)

Part of full recovery and restoring joy is found when we make a covenant with God. This is an intimate promise between you and God made with sincerity and focused on Him. No one can force you to make a covenant with God but it can be a very important step toward forgiveness and recovery. The covenant with God allows a clearing of your conscience but note that not only does the Spirit validate your clear conscience; the Spirit also "convicts the guilty conscience" (Moore, 2001, p. 193). This means as you begin to recognize and admit your guilt, God will work on your heart to help you see the need to confess the sin as you ask God to remove the negative power it has over you. As he cleanses your past, you are ready to move toward inner peace.

Discussion Points

Because following Christ is a choice and because we all need to recognize our own responsibility for the sins we commit, take time to reflect on the areas in your life where personal growth is needed. This exercise is designed to help you clear your conscience and feel better about the events of which you took part and how to begin to remove guilt-ridden thoughts from your mind. Think privately about times you found yourself in trouble and were not taking full responsibility for the actions that led to the difficulty. Fill in each part of the missing information based on your personal experience:

a. The last time I made a decision that caused me difficulty was when I:

b. The emotions I felt most strongly during the experience were:

c. My actions could be described as:

d. The results of this decision were:

e. In order to clear my conscience, I need to:

f. If I could do it all over again I would change:

Prayer

Father in Heaven, this is so hard. We are coming to You at this time to ask for forgiveness for the things that have caused us to fall away from You. The guilt and shame we have experienced is crippling and has caused us to be less than You have wanted for us. We recognize our part in the damage that has been done to ourselves and to those we care about. Please help us to be able to admit our guilt as we recognize sin for what it is. We ask You to walk with us and hold us accountable for the decisions we make in the future and as we falter from time to time we ask that You remind us of Your undying love for us and give us strength. Help us to make good decisions that bring light into our world as we grow more closely to You. In Jesus' name we pray, Amen

Finding Peace Through Emotional Healing

> Therefore, since we have been justified through faith, we have peace with God through our Lord Jesus Christ. Romans 5:1

In my vast studies of Scripture and of Bible teachers, I found that Stormie Omartian shared a great deal of understanding of a woman's heart. She was able to put into words the feelings of pain I have experienced while searching for God's purpose in my own life. Although the following definition was also shared earlier in this book, I felt it should be repeated in this section. In her book <u>Lord, I Want to be Whole</u>, she provided a definition for emotional health that allowed me to reach my own understanding of how to feel complete in my search for God. Her definition of emotional health is as follows:

> Having total peace about who you are, what you are doing, and where you are going, both individually and in relationship with those around you. It's feeling totally at peace about the past, the present, and the future of your life. It's knowing that you are in line with God's ultimate purpose for you—and being fulfilled in that. (2001, p. 3)

The Life Application Bible (NIV, 2005) explains in Isaiah, "Because he has saved us, we can trust him and be peacefully confident that he will give us strength to face our difficulties. We should lay aside our busy care and endless effort to allow him to act" (p. 1124). In this message is the hope that brings about emotional peace if we will simply, or not so simply, lay to rest our own desires to be in charge. "Peace comes when we relinquish ownership of what we face to the One who has unlimited ability, inexhaustible resources, and impeccable timing" (Mayes, 1995, p. 191). Instead, relax and rest in knowing God has you in the palm of His hand and will not allow you to fall once you have found peace in His promise to you.

In all likelihood, there are people who would give anything to feel peace in their daily lives. I imagine there are even very wealthy people who thought money would buy anything they ever wanted, except we know peace does not have monetary value. True peace is found only when we commit ourselves to God and His purpose for us. "Peace can be experienced only when we have received divine pardon—when we have been reconciled to God and when we have harmony within, with our fellow man and especially with God" (Graham, 1984, p. 267).

Discussion Points

To help us look deeper into our personal understanding of emotional health, use the following guidelines to help you walk through a better understanding of where you are in your own emotional health. Within this walk, look at how inner peace is affected based on what you are experiencing at the moment. Use the definition of peace as; "a state of calm; freedom from strife or discord; harmony in personal relationship" (Life Application Study Bible, NIV, 2005, p. 2353).

a. List the times and situations in your past when you felt most at peace:

What physical reactions were you experiencing?

b. List the times and situations in your past when you felt stress and uncertainty:

What physical reactions were you experiencing?

c. Describe what is going on in your life right now when you feel most at peace:

d. Describe what is going on in your life right now that causes you to feel uncertainty or stress.

e. As you think about the future, what do you believe is needed in your life to feel at peace?

> f. What fears do you experience that may cause you to worry about the future?
>
> g. What steps can you take to find peace in your daily activities?

Prayer

Precious Heavenly Father, we thank You for the times of peace within our lives. We thank You for sending your son to save us from a world of sin and destruction. Remind us daily of His willingness to guide us in all of our comings and our goings as we learn to develop emotional peace. Help us to find the purpose You have for us while we learn to listen for Your voice as our guide and protector. We ask for opportunities and wisdom to find peace in our daily lives so that we may focus on the love You have for us. In Your son's name we pray, Amen.

Peace with Obedience

> Whatever you have learned or received or heard from
> me, or seen in me—put it into practice. And the God
> of peace will be with you. Philippians 4:9

As we think about the peace we crave in our lives, uncomplicated precious peace, we have to realize it is easier than we can even imagine. All we need to do to experience the soothing calm of inner peace is to say yes to God when He calls us to Him. When we learn to follow Him as shown in the Bible and in the workings of Jesus, we will find that the trust we place upon Him in our obedience, becomes our raft of safety in the tumultuous rivers of life. Christ gently holds us in His heart and wraps His arms around us with peace and comfort. It is the desire to care for us that allows Him to become our peace; He is the gentle promise that whispers unconditional love and acceptance. Terkeurst (2007) explained it this way:

> In our world of turmoil and uncertainty, there is nothing more precious than peace. When we say yes to God we know that our life and the lives of those we love rest in the certainty of His never-changing love for us. While we can't control the circumstances we face, we can choose how we react to them. If you've settled in your heart to say yes to God and completely trust Him, then you don't have to worry about the future. You are not in charge of the outcome; you are simply responsible to be obedient. You will be blessed with the peace of knowing that God has a perfect plan and holds everything in His perfect control. What freedom this brings! (p. 145)

Bringing peace to your own life is something to strive for on a daily basis. Begin by saying yes to what God is calling you to do. He does not call all people to do the same things and what He calls you to do is your opportunity to serve Him in that calling. It may be something as simple as reading to the elderly, writing letters to soldiers, or taking cookies to a shut-in. God just wants you to experience the love He has for you by your own actions of love for others. Watch and listen for Him to give you direction and then plan to be obedient to His Word by learning more about what He calls all of us to do in His name.

As we continue to learn about inner peace through obedience we can learn about our call to obedience as found in Scripture. Such as Paul wrote in Romans 1:5, "Through him and for his namesake, we received grace and apostleship to call people from among all the Gentiles to the obedience that comes from faith." Through study of this Scripture we learn that God asks us to represent Him and to show others the good works He is doing in us. To be obedient we are not to hide what He has done for us but rather be willing to tell anyone and everyone about the changes we are experiencing by being obedient to His calling. Then in 1 Peter 1:14-16, we read, "As obedient children, do not conform to the evil desires you had when you lived in ignorance. But just as he who called you is holy, so be holy in all you do, for it is written: 'Be holy, because I am holy.' This Scripture is explained in the Life Application Bible (NIV, 2005), as:

> He is a God of mercy and justice who cares personally for each of his followers. Our holy God expects us to imitate him by following his high moral standards. Like him, we should be both merciful and just; like him, we should sacrifice ourselves for others. (p. 2103)

To reach the ideal levels of mercy and sacrifice for others, we will need to put away the old habits and poor decisions that have led us astray. To be as close to the ways of Christ as we can be will provide a byproduct of inner peace. The plan for our daily living should include looking for ways to be obedient to the laws God has set before us. When we are faced with a difficult decision or a temptation to revert back to some of our bad habits, we should consider the choices we have and decide if our decision would be pleasing to Christ? Lutzer writes about developing a union with Christ to help alleviate the temptations or old habits that plague us. He wrote:

> This union with Christ is the basis for transforming our lifestyle and desires. Despite our struggles and failures, we must not think of ourselves as sinners or as addicts but rather as redeemed people joined to Christ for a life of spiritual freedom and personal holiness. If we can keep in mind who we actually are—that is, as being "in Christ"—we can withstand the attacks of temptation more easily. We will see ourselves as those who no longer need to obey the desires of the flesh, for we have a new relationship and spiritual identity. (2001, pp. 204-205)

Discussion Points

There is much written in the Bible about peaceful living and God's desire that we find peace in our relationships. Use the following Scriptures to help you address your own understanding of God's plan for peace in your life.

- I have no peace, no quietness; I have no rest, but only turmoil. Job 3:26
- The Lord gives strength to his people; the Lord blesses his people with peace. Psalm 29:11
- Turn from evil and do good; seek peace and pursue it. Psalm 34:14

- Consider the blameless, observe the upright; there is a future for the man of peace. Psalm 37:37
- The fruit of righteousness will be peace; the effect of righteousness will be quietness and confidence forever. Isaiah 32:17
- The mind of sinful man is death, but the mind controlled by the Spirit is life and peace. Romans 8:6
- But the fruit of the Spirit is love, joy, peace, patience, kindness, goodness, faithfulness, gentleness, and self-control. Galatians 6:22
- Make every effort to live in peace with all men and to be holy; without holiness no one will see the Lord. Hebrews 12:14

a. Which of the Scriptures listed above speaks closest to your own experiences?

b. Which of the Scriptures help you have hope as you seek peace for yourself and your situation? Why?

d. When you read the Scriptures consider how obedience correlates with peace?

e. What do you feel God is saying to you personally within the above Scriptures?

Prayer

Father God we ask that You come to us today in this place. Help us to hear Your voice through the message we receive through Scripture and reflection. We ask that You guide us through Your written Word as we lean on Your promises to be with us in all things. Help us to develop a promised peace within our lives so that we may find strength to follow You more closely. In Your son's name, Amen.

Removing Fear

> Say to those with fearful hearts, "Be strong, do not fear; your God will come, he will come with vengeance; with divine retribution he will come to save you." Isaiah 35:4

Being fearful or afraid can be an unbearable condition and can block our ability to feel the peace God has promised. Fear can be so paralyzing that it causes people to withdraw from any contact with others and to avoid any situation that may place them outside of their own comfort zone. For women living with addictions or self-destructive behaviors, fear can present itself as a roadblock to recovery. To be afraid often means a feeling of aloneness where the world feels too big and frightening to be a part of it. This kind of crippling fear can be a catalyst for introducing dangerous methods that mask the fear. Masking the fear is done in an attempt to cope with the challenges of life that are causing the fear in the first place and may include using drugs or alcohol to block the memory or face reality. Recovery may mean facing fears that have caused the individual to make decisions that have affected life long relationships and physical well-being. Addressing those things that lead a person to be afraid may be the first step in finding peace and contentment. It is important to keep in mind, however, that those who are living in fear may need professional help to address the root cause of the fear before healing can take place.

Being afraid is something we do not always admit to when discussing a relationship with God. He can seem very frightening to us if we are just coming to know Him on a personal level. The unknown is always a bit frightening and for someone who has not grown up in the church or has not had healthy relationships with professed God-loving people, their view of God may be very distorted or even frightening. We can feel afraid He will not accept us; we may become fearful that He will harshly punish us for our sins; we may feel He is too distant to really hear our cry for help; we may become afraid that it is too late for redemption and we are destined for hell. When someone shares a fear, it is very real to him or her and should not be judged in any way. One person's fear may seem very trivial to some, but to those of us experiencing fear, it is huge and may be the roadblock to full recovery. Never underestimate the control that fear can have over a person who is working through personal demons or facing the results of life-altering experiences. God does not want us to be afraid, not of Him or of His plans for us. He is ready at all times to remove the fear from our hearts and set us free. This may be the time when we need to fall on our knees and place the fear at the foot of the cross and trust Jesus to raise us up under the light of His protective presence.

Fear is an emotion that can lead to physical ailments as well as behaviors that cause us to emotionally fade away from society or from our own families. It is an emotion that can be paralyzing in every way. If we are to be fully healed from brokenness, it means we must trust God to take away the fear and hopelessness that often accompanies the brokenness. Much of the fears we experience develop from memories we have either relived over and over or suppressed so as not to have to relive the trauma. Yeager (2012) wrote,

> Our memories are very powerful and come back to us at times with strong emotions. Emotions are indicators that there are issues still going on underneath. Sometimes there are parts of the pain that we are not dealing with and it is "piling up" unnoticed. When we are in the process of healing sometimes we hurt before we are healed. We have to make it through the pain in order to receive the gift of healing. (p. 118)

Although fear can be powerful and controlling, we can certainly remove it from our lives, but only by using God's power to do so. Trust Him to do the work for you. He will take the fear from you and replace it with peace and joy that will allow you to move forward. Take the past fears and use them to help you develop empathy and understanding for those around you who are facing what you have already worked through. Just understand that it takes time to reach the personal peace you desire through the inner healing you are working toward.

The following Scriptures provide biblical support for the principle of fear.

- When I am afraid, I will trust in you. In God, whose Word I praise, in God I trust; I will not be afraid. What can mortal man do to me? Psalm 56:3-4
- Do not tremble, do not be afraid. Did I not proclaim this and foretell it long ago? You are my witnesses. Is there any God besides me? No, there is no other Rock; I know not one. Isaiah 44:8

- Do not be afraid of them, for I am with you and will rescue you, declares the Lord. Jeremiah 1:8
- . . . Jesus told the synagogue ruler, Don't be afraid; just believe. Mark 5:36
- Peace I leave with you; my peace I give you. I do not give to you as the world gives. Do not let your hearts be troubled and do not be afraid. John 14:27
- So we say with confidence, the Lord is my helper; I will not be afraid. What can man do to me? Hebrews 13:6

Discussion Points

Review the Scriptures listed above and think about how fear has limited your ability to feel God's presence in your life. When reflecting on the words provided in the Scriptures, determine how you can apply them to your situation in a way that will help you remove the power of fear in your life. Because fear can destroy emotional strength, think about how you can begin to trust God to remove the fear you experience. Use the following questions to help you work through your thoughts on fear and how you may come to feel personal peace.

a. When do you find yourself most afraid of your circumstances?

b. What is the first thing you do when you are consumed by fear?

c. What does it mean to you to when you read Scripture that asks, "what can mortal man do to me?"

d. Where do you feel least afraid and does this happen when you are with another person or when you are alone?

e. Which of the Scriptures listed above speak to you personally and how does it relate to what you are feeling now?

f. What steps can you take to begin to turn your fear over to God so that you may develop inner peace?

Prayer

Heavenly Father, we come today with a thankful heart as we feel Your presence in our lives. Although there are times when we do not always hear Your voice, we know You have not given up on us. As each day passes we want to be reminded that You are with us at all times and we do not need to be filled with fear. Please keep us strong and help us to always find those who love You to help us keep steadfast in our recovery. We want to feel completely free and to follow Your plan for us as we experience personal peace and inner healing. Thank You for Your faithfulness. We pray this in Your name, Amen.

<u>Leader Notes</u>: Edward Anton wrote, "God grieves over his children who sit in the darkness of sin, devoid of peace. Our failures to repent sadden him" (2005, p. 65). Recovery is a process and can involve change or alternation of our emotional health. As we face physical and emotional changes when looking at recovery methods, when addressing addictions, there will ultimately be times of pain and sorrow. It is never easy to give up something that has given us comfort, even if destructive and short-lived comfort. People who are living with addictions or personal trauma are likely to need time to develop the skills needed to fight against the control of the addiction, habit, or poor choices. Those struggling to recover from a debilitating issue may slip backward from time to time until they find their footing and develop the inner strength and trust in God as the deliverer. Falling back does not mean recovery will not happen, it means more time and patience is needed. As God never gives up on us, we should never give up on someone who is searching for the path to recovery. Part of the recovery process involves finding peace through God's grace and mercy. Encouragement that helps someone to find significance in relationship with Him is an imperative part of the recovery effort. "For I know the plans I have for you, declares the Lord, plans to prosper you and not to harm you, plans to give you hope and a future" (Jeremiah 29:11).

Freedom

> Then you will know the truth, and the truth will set you free. John 8:32

The definition of freedom used in the Life Application Bible (NIV, 2005) states, "voluntary; without restraint; without cost; to set at liberty" (p. 2330). The feeling of freedom comes when recovery has occurred and we are willing to continue to follow God's plan rather than trying to make decisions or live a life void of His presence. Dr. Jeremiah wrote, "The journey of recovery starts here and nowhere. You've got to own up to what you've done" (2001, p. 78). Acknowledging the sin(s) is step one if you intend to travel the path to freedom from the burdens your carry. True recovery will come with a sense of freedom only after the work is done. As we find in the fifth chapter of Galatians and explained in the Life Application Bible:

> Christ came to set us free—not free to do whatever we want because that would lead us back into slavery to our selfish desires. Rather, thanks to Christ, we are now free and are able to do what was impossible before—to live unselfishly. Those who appeal to their freedom so that they can have their own way or indulge in their own desires are falling back into sin. (NIV, 2005, p. 1974)

For the purpose of our work together, we can take the concept of freedom and apply it to the freedom from addiction or any behavior causing uncontrolled harmful or hurtful habits. Anything that consumes us physically or emotionally and leads to destruction is an area whereby freedom may be desired. Anyone held captive by destructive behaviors are those who have fallen away from personal peace, emotional and physical health, and healthy relationships that only God can provide. Such peace is not attainable alone. Turning to man's methods and abilities to provide happiness and safety will only mask the true peace found through God's undying love. It is about choice. God gives us a choice to follow Him or to go it alone. He will not interfere with your personal desires but He will be ready to embrace you when you are willing to be obedient to His purpose.

The following Scriptures may be used to address the area of freedom:

- It is for freedom that Christ has set us free. Stand firm, then, and do not let yourselves be burdened again by a yoke of slavery. Galatians 5:1
- If anyone is in Christ, he is a new creation; the old has gone, the new has come. 2 Corinthians 5:17
- To the Jews who had believed him, Jesus said, "if you hold to my teaching, you are really my disciples. Then you will know the truth, and the truth will set you free." John 8:31-32
- For we know that our old self was crucified with him so that the body of sin might be done away with, that we should no longer be slaves to sin—because anyone who has died has been freed from sin. Romans 6:6-7
- Now the Lord is the Spirit, and where the Spirit of the Lord is, there is freedom. 2 Corinthians 3:17

Discussion Points

Because recovery is ongoing and often feels like an *uphill battle*, there are things that can be done to help ensure recovery is realized on a daily basis. First read through the Scriptures listed above and reflect on what each verse means to you. The following information and questions will help you understand the meaning behind the Scripture. This is something that can be repeated over time to help you stay true to the course of long lasting recovery. These Scriptures are a reminder that to be set free does not mean we are free to do whatever we wish. Instead, we are to follow God's laws knowing that His requirements for us are not to make life difficult, but rather to help us become more like Christ. Without following Christ, we fall back into slavery, which is the sin that has held us captive.

Scripture #1: It is for freedom that Christ has set us free. Stand firm, then, and do not let yourselves be burdened again by a yoke of slavery. Galatians 5:1

> a. When you think of God's laws, what do you feel He is asking of us?
>
> b. How can you be more like Christ in your daily walk?
>
> c. What does falling back into slavery mean to you personally?

Scripture #2: If anyone is in Christ, he is a new creation; the old has gone, the new has come. 2 Corinthians 5:17

a. What does it mean to be *in Christ*?

b. How do/will you feel as a *new creation*?

c. How will you know when the *old has gone* and the *new has come*?

Scripture #3: To the Jews who had believed him, Jesus said, "if you hold to my teaching, you are really my disciples. Then you will know the truth, and the truth will set you free." John 8:31-32

a. What does it mean to you to be a disciple of Christ?

b. What truth is Jesus talking about in this Scripture?

c. How will knowing the truth *set you free*?

Scripture #4: For we know that our old self was crucified with him so that the body of sin might be done away with, that we should no longer be slaves to sin—because anyone who has died has been freed from sin. Romans 6:6-7

a. Explain what the Scripture means by our old self was *crucified with him.*

b. What sin holds or has held you captive?

c. What does it mean we need to die to be free from sin?

Scripture # 5: Now the Lord is the Spirit, and where the Spirit of the Lord is, there is freedom. 2 Corinthians 3:17

a. What does this Scripture say to you personally?

b. When do you feel the presence of the spirit in your own life?

c. When do you feel most free? Explain the feeling of freedom, as you know it to be.

Prayer

Dear Heavenly Father. We know that Jesus said that the truth will set you free and since we believe in His teaching, we know this is true. Thank You for coming to us each day to guide our thoughts and hold our hearts close to You as we learn more about freedom from those things that have held us captive for so long. Bring us closer to You, Lord, each day and remind us of Your presence. Help us to remember that the truth is only found in You and we must have an intimate relationship with You so that we will one day be with You in Heaven. In Your holy name we pray, Amen.

Now What?

> You need to persevere so that when you have done the will of God, you will receive what he has promised.
> Hebrews 10:36

Recovery is an ongoing process for anyone who has experienced life-controlling events such as addictions with drugs, alcohol, or any unhealthy lifestyle. Completing a Bible study is an excellent beginning but not the end of the journey. Anyone who has experienced a life of poor decision-making that has resulted in addiction, or anything that has caused a captive life style, will need to consider the next steps to ensure they stay strong in the Word and continue to fight against Satan's desire to win them back to a life of destruction. It is now about perseverance, which means you do not give up on yourself or on what God is calling you to do. You continue to fight for your life in Christ without giving up. The following ideas may be considered to help promote a life of continued freedom. The following list is adapted from

Kern's small group study book entitled <u>Live Free Journey: Small Group Study</u> (2009, p. 94). As you are ready to look at next steps for your growth, consider the following:

- Know where you are in your journey as you end the group study. Have a conversation with someone you trust to explore how to keep moving forward and growing deeper in your understanding of God's plan for your life.
- Network with other group members and with strong, supportive people who can commit to encouraging you on a regular basis.
- Create or join a new ongoing group that meets at least one time per month for continual encouragement as you learn to live a life of freedom.
- Ask for recommendations of resources to strengthen your relationship with God. Enhance your ability to get to know Him more deeply through prayer and the study of Scripture.
- Continue to involve yourself in ministry by serving and using your strengths and talents.
- Keep in mind that transformation is a lifestyle. We all need continued encouragement, support, and challenge to keep any new lifestyle commitments going. It is vital to nurture what God has begun to do in your life.
- Find a church family who will give you Godly advice and then become involved in the activities of the church. Be sure the church is a Bible teaching church.

There will be times when we find it difficult, if not impossible, to stay on the path to follow Christ in our lives. A life altering habit is not easily given up and Satan will do everything he can to stop us from succeeding. However, Satan should not be used as an excuse as to why failure to change occurs. We are blessed that God is more powerful than Satan and will intervene on our behalf when we call out to Him for help. He will not force us to follow Him but He will never give up on waiting for us to make the commitment to believe in Him. Perseverance is the key element when trying to make change. It is about facing the dark, but choosing to walk in the light. It is about saying no to people and temptations that put us in unhealthy environments. It is about looking up with a prayer on our lips and a desire to receive the blessing of freedom from that which has held us captive far too long.

I am not suggesting that major change is easy to accomplish. On the contrary, when Satan has had part or all of you for any period of time, the change will be perhaps the most difficult struggle you have ever experienced. Far too many people give up and feel it is too hard to manage alone. Please remember, you are not alone! God is with you at all times, through your faith in Him and through the love and support from people who love and care for you. Hunt (2011) explains the challenge of struggling by those who have decided to become new people in Christ. She wrote:

> Because strugglers experience so many failed attempts at dealing with their addictions, friends and family sometimes find it hard to stay closely connected. They experience frustration and despair as the struggler, inconceivably to them, falls yet another time. It may take decades of prayer and a thousand false starts, but we are to continue to pray for our strugglers—no matter what they do or don't do. The Bible says, "As for me, far be it from me that I should sin against the Lord by failing to pray for you" (Samuel 12:23).

Hunt is not suggesting that everyone will fail. Instead we are reminded that it is possible some strugglers will continue to fail for a while. Those of us who wish to help someone reach a life of freedom should be there to pray and not give up on them. This means that the person wanting change should not give up on himself or herself either. We may need to be reminded to be diligent and pick ourselves up and start again any time we fall back. "Complete victory is possible—not only in the perfection we'll know in heaven, but right here in our fallen, imperfect world. This victory comes to us through the limitless power of Christ" (Hunt, p. 385). Will it be difficult? Sure it will! Making change of the heart is very hard, but not as difficult when that change includes an invitation for God to enter into your life and show you the way you are to go. As we learn in II Peter 1:3-4, "His divine power has given us everything we need for life and godliness through our knowledge of him who called us by his own glory and goodness. Through these he has given us his very great and precious promises, so that through them you may participate in the divine nature and escape the corruption in the world cased by evil desires."

Discussion Points

As we come to an end of our Bible study, it is by no means the end of the journey. The following questions will help form a plan to follow so that you will be more likely to stay on the path to recovery. I remind you to always pray earnestly for God to guide you in all situations. Read the following information and determine a plan for future work during your journey toward personal peace and inner healing.

a. A support group or person will be your lifeline to help hold you accountable to God's plan for you. Seek out mature Christian women who can serve as your life coaches and help you continue moving in the path of faithful living.

   1. Name one person you would like to ask to be a prayer partner with you: Someone who you can trust with confidential discussions.

   2. When will you approach this person?

   3. What will you ask them specifically?

b. Spending time reading and studying your Bible will be instrumental in your growth as a follower of Christ. Try to acquire a study Bible so that you have more information provided as you study and learn about what God is calling you to do.

   1. If you have a Bible, which one will you use? If not, when will you work on finding one to use?

2. What time of day will be the best time for you
to read in your Bible? How much time do you
think you can give to the daily reading?

3. Which book of the Bible or topic would you
like to study first?

c. To help remain accountable to what God is asking
of you and to develop Christian friendships,
attending church will be a good place to find what
you need. Not all churches are the same. Ask about
visiting with someone you trust and whom you
know is a believer. Check the church website to
determine if they have support groups or other
resources that would benefit your personal needs.
Be sure the church you choose is a Bible believing
church.

1. Who do you think you could ask about visiting
their church? If you already attend a church,
who at this church do you think you could
ask to help pray with you about your need to
continue your growth in the Lord?

2. When looking at a church website, what will you specifically look for as far as programs that will help support your growth? If you already have a church, what programs are offered that may help you become more spiritually involved?

d. As you continue to become the person that you know God wants you to be, think about the barriers and roadblocks that will cause some difficulty in your recovery progress.

   1. What may be the most difficult thing for you to change before emotional and spiritual healing can be accomplished? How do you plan to begin to face that difficulty?

   2. What will you need to do first to begin the process of healthy living? Who is the first person you will need to talk to about this plan?

   3. Who do you trust among your family or friends to show you unconditional love without judgment as you take the first steps toward recovery?

Prayer

Our dear Heavenly Father, we are so thankful for all You provide for us as we learn to know You more deeply. Thank you for always being just a breath away. Help us to continue our journey of restoration by finding the people and places in our lives that will allow us to continue our growth. Help us to know how to work for You by showing us how to develop the gifts and talents You have given to us as Your disciples. Please send Godly people into the lives of those who do not yet know You or who are running from You. Help them to discover the healing power of your love. In Your son's name we pray, Amen.

Leader Notes: As the study comes to a conclusion, some women will feel anxiety about beginning the journey alone. Help them to be assured that you will always be available for prayer as they step out in faith. You may need to help give them some ideas regarding the above questions as they make their plan to begin a personal recovery process. As I have mentioned before, you may want to have contacts available for those who would like to seek some professional support in the future.

A Thankful Heart

> Speak to one another with psalms, hymns and spiritual songs. Sing and make music in your heart to the Lord, always giving thanks to God the Father for everything in the name of our Lord Jesus Christ. Ephesians 5:19-20

The final step in this study is to share your thankful heart with God for the work He has done in you. Learning to recognize His love is paramount in your ability to understand all that He has done to draw you closer to Him. From that realization you will begin to share His love with others as a follower of Christ. Your personal growth will create in you a new spirit, a spirit of love and understanding for God's people. Your relationship with Christ will provide strength and wisdom that will help you become a better friend, daughter, parent, or spouse. You will become a worthy example to others as you emulate Christ in action.

Now is the time to fully embrace all that He has done for you. As we have discussed before, it is very important to praise God in all things. He is the creator of our world and is in control of every thing that happens. He wants the best for all of us and is ready to celebrate victory found in freedom when we are ready to work through all of the issues that have slowed down our recovery. He is ready to celebrate with you and welcome you into the kingdom. Reach within yourself and discover the joy that is in your heart, the peace that is yours to embrace, and the inner healing that is now your new life. Share your thankful heart with the God of all people who has brought you closer to Him.

Discussion Points

Take time to write a personal prayer that asks God what you are to do next. Thank Him for what you have experienced that has been helpful to your recovery of a changed life and share with Him how you plan to further your efforts to become His child and to live the life He has chosen for you. To help you develop this prayer, fill in each section. After you have done that, read the prayer to yourself and see if it covers everything your heart wants to express.

Section #1: Thank God for what He has done for you that has been helpful to your life change goals.

Section #2: Ask God for guidance for what He is asking you to do next, so that you stay on the right path.

Section #3: Share with God what you are committed to do so that personal growth continues. Ask God to help you with this plan.

In Jesus' name I pray, Amen

Prayer

Our Father God in Heaven, we thank You for the blessings You have given to each of us throughout this Bible study. We thank You for not giving up on us even when some of our topics caused discomfort and fear. We trust You with all of our hearts and know that You want only the very best for each of us. Help us as we go out and use what we have learned to grow even closer to You. Help us to hear Your voice each day through our prayers, our study, and our family and friends. Help us to recognize You in all things and give us strength to avoid the barriers that may trip us up from time to time. Remind us that You are all powerful and the only way to full recovery. Remind us to always have a thankful heart for the blessings You provide for us. In Your blessed name we pray, Amen.

Conclusion

Recovery is a far-reaching topic when we think about the different problems women face that lead to a life of emotional captivity. Much of the emotional elements of captivity lead to physical problems therefore both must be addressed. This chapter spoke a lot about finding emotional peace, which included looking at clearing a conscience. This is an area that can be difficult for women who feel terribly guilty about their past or how they have hurt other people, even if they are not totally responsible for the negative action. Our emotions play a huge part in how we look at the world and how we relate to those we love. Women living in crisis situations may have difficulty understanding how God could love them when they have not found a way to love themselves. Looking at obedience to God's commands can be a tough road to travel when the women in the group have lived a life of disobedience, not only to God, but also to the world in general. It is part of a survival technique for many women to fight against authority in all things. To feel completely free from the oppression of unhealthy life styles and unhealthy relationships, each woman will need to seek help from others around her. She will most likely struggle some along the way but when she is able to walk away from the things in life that cause her to go back to the source of the problems, she is more likely to develop an inner strength to move on. By finding a church home or at least Christian support through Godly people, she will be more likely to improve her skill set for making good decisions and living the life that God has planned for her all along.

FINAL THOUGHTS

A Letter to Women Who Serve Those Living in Crisis

O ne of my favorite verses comes from Romans 12:2, "Do not change yourselves to be like the people of this world, but be changed within by a new way of thinking. Then you will be able to decide what God wants for you; you will know what is good and pleasing to Him and what is perfect."

If you have decided to step out in faith and lead a group of women who are searching for God's voice, then I want to personally thank you for following your heart in this way. As you are likely aware, all of us have an obligation to do what God is calling us to do. He does not expect everyone to do the big things in our Christian walk, but He does expect us to use the gifts He has given us and to find the path of understanding; that being the plan He has for His children. If you feel called to work with women held captive by the negativity of the world and the decisions that have lead to crisis in their lives, then you have answered God's call to do what you can to bring His children to Him. You will realize no woman who enters your group will be in the same place in their Christian growth at the same time. Patience and understanding will be instrumental in the success of your program but only if you make an effort to not judge and base all of what you do on Scripture and the teachings of Christ. A scriptural example of those who found it easy to forget to put God first in order to avoid falling back into bad habits comes from the seventh book of Jeremiah, verses 21-23, where we learn about why God called people to perform a sacrifice to Him. We learn that God was not interested in the sacrifice itself but the obedience of the people to focus on Him and not on their usual life styles that were not of God's pleasing. God asked for the ritual of sacrifice to call the people to Him and to remind them why they were performing the sacrifice in the first place. "They followed the stubborn inclinations of their evil hearts. They went backward and not forward" (Jeremiah 7:24). This Scripture reiterates the inclination of mankind to avoid serving God with a propensity to behave according to what feels personally satisfying, which often causes some to fall back into old habits instead of moving steadily forward. As we seek to honor God by using the skills and talents He has given us, we are holding ourselves accountable to His calling. We are called to keep our eye on Him in all things of this life. This is a lesson that may be difficult for some women to follow when they are controlled by a life-altering substance or unhealthy choices.

Martin Luther once said, "God created the world out of nothing, and as long as we are nothing, He can make something out of us" (as cited in Voskamp, 2010). This quote speaks to the hearts of women who struggle each day to face the challenges and concerns they have for themselves and their families. To fully embrace a sinful nature is difficult and uncomfortable but can be accomplished through the promises God has made His people since the beginning of time. To lead others does not mean you have all of the answers nor does it mean you have led a perfect life. It means you are a seeker and willing to submit yourself to God's request to use your gifts to help others find their way. You will not always experience victories and will certainly have your heart broken as you watch some women struggle and fight against what God wants for them. However, your strength to endure will come from the Holy Spirit breathing God's power in you. Take what you learn as you lead and apply it to each situation that God sends to you. Do not give up, God gave you a passion for a reason and it is your job to use that passion to reach as many hurting women as you can. As I shared in the final chapter, "Complete victory is possible—not only in the perfection we'll know in heaven, but right here in our fallen, imperfect world. This victory comes to us through the limitless power of Christ" (Hunt, 2011, p. 385).

It has been my great honor to write this book as a message from God for women to use as an individual Bible study or for other women like you, who feel God is calling them to serve Him by serving others. It is my prayer that you will find the information helpful and supportive for your journey into the challenges that I promise will befall you. May God light your path, warm your heart, and bring you joy in serving Him.

In His service,
Dr. Patricia Allison

DEFINITIONS

Addiction: Addictions are a compulsive, enslaving dependence on something, resulting in detrimental patterns of thinking and behaving. There are *substance addictions* (e.g. alcohol, tobacco, heroin, inhalants) and *process addictions* (e.g. gambling, eating, shopping, sex) (Hunt, 2011, p. 25).

Alcoholism: A complete dependence on alcohol consumption. (Symtomfind.com, 2013)

Anorexia: A eating disorder characterized by compulsive, chronic self-starvation with a refusal to maintain a body weight within 15 percent of a person's normal weight. (American Psychiatric Association, 2002)

Bulimia: A psychological eating disorder characterized by repeated or sporadic "binge and purge" episodes. (Mayo Clinic, 2010)

Doubt: To lack confidence in; uncertainty. (Life Application Study Bible, NIV, 2005, p. 2323)

Faith: Reliance, loyalty, or complete trust in God or someone else (Life Application Study Bible, NIV, 2005, p. 2326)

Forgiveness: To pardon or acquit of sins; acquittal (Life Application Study Bible, NIV, 2005, p. 2329)

Freedom: Voluntary; without restraint; without cost; to set at liberty (Life Application Bible, NIV, 2005, p. 2330)

Guilt: Being responsible for an offense or wrongdoing (Life Application Study Bible, NIV, 2005, p. 2334).

Habit: A pattern of behavior acquired by frequent repetition. (Global Strategy on /diet, Physical Activity and Health: Obesity and Overweight, as cited by Hunt, 2011, p. 27)

Peace: State of calm; freedom from strife or discord; harmony in personal relationship. (Life Application Study Bible, NIV, 2005, p. 2353)

Redemption: To buy back, repurchase; to rescue (often from sin) with a ransom (price paid for release from captivity) (Life Application Study Bible, NIV, 2005, pp. 2358-2359)

Repentance: To experience sorrow for and seek to change wrong behavior (Life Application Study Bible, NIV, 2005, p. 2359)

Reconciliation: To restore harmony between persons (Life Application Study Bible, NIV, 2005, p. 2359).

Recovery: The process of combating a disorder (as alcoholism) or a real or perceived problem. (Merriam-Webster.com, 2013)

Salvation: Deliverance from danger or difficulty; deliverance from the power of penalty of sin (Life Application Bible, NIV, 2005, p. 2361).

Sin: Violation of conscience or of divine law; missing he mark; falling short of God's perfect standard. (Life Application Study Bible, NIV, 2005, p. 2364)

Substance Abuse: The use of a chemical—legal or illegal—to the extent that the usage causes physical, mental, or emotional harm (Baker Encyclopedia of Psychology, 1985).

REFERENCES

Alcoholism and alcohol abuse. (n.d.). Retrieved from http://helpguide.org/mental/alcohol_abuse_alcoholism_signs_effects_treatment.htm

Anton, E. J. (2005). *Repentance: A cosmic shift of mind & heart.* Waltham, MA: Discipleship Publications International.

Brown, S. (1992). *Overcoming setbacks: jumping hurdles, hitting glitches.* Colorado Springs, CO: NAVPRESS

Comfort, R. (2010). *God has a wonderful plan for your life: The myth of the modern message.* Bellflower, CA: Living Waters Publication

Cymbala, J. (2003). *Break through prayer.* Grand Rapids, MI: Zondervan

DeMoss, N. L. (2001). *Lies women believe: And the truth that sets them free.* Chicago, Ill: Moody Publishers

Graham, B. (1984). *Peace with God.* W. Publishing Group

Heald, C. (2000). *Becoming a woman of faith.* Nashville, TN: Thomas Nelson Publishers

Holderread-Heggen, C., Shenk-Keener, R., & Lapp-Guengerich, R. (2011). *Sister care: Equipping women for caring ministry.* Newton, KS: Mennonite Women USA

Holladay, T. (2008). *The relationship principles of Jesus.* Grand Rapids, MI: Zondervan

Hunt, J. (2011). *How to defeat harmful habits: Freedom from six addictive behaviors.* Eugene, OR: Harvest House.

Indermark, J. (2006). *Parables and passions: Jesus' stories for the days of lent.* Nashville, TN: Upper Room Books.

Jeremiah, D. (1998). *God in you: Releasing the power of the Holy Spirit in your life.* Orange, CA: Multnomah Publishers

Jeremiah, D. (2001). *Slaying the giants in your life: You can win the battle and live victoriously.* Nashville, TN: Thomas Nelson

Jeremiah, D. (2012). *God loves you: He always has-he always will.* New York, NY: Faith Words.

Kendall, R. T. (2002). *Total forgiveness.* Lake Mary, Florida: Charisma House

Kern, J. (2009). *Live free journey: Small group study.* Cincinnati, OH: Standard Publishing

Life application study Bible. (2005). New International Version. Carol Stream, IL: Tyndale House Publisher

Life application study Bible. (1996). New Kings James Version. Carol Stream, IL: Tyndale House Publisher

Lucado, M. (1998). *God's roadmap for new beginnings: Let the journey begin.* Nashville, TN: Thomas Nelson, Inc.

Lutzer, E. W. (2001). *Seven snares of the enemy: Breaking free from the devil's grip.* Chicago, Illinois: Moody Press

Mayes, G. R. (1995). *Now what: Resting in the Lord when life doesn't make sense.* Wheaton, Ill: Crossbooks

Meyer, J. (2011). *Battlefield of the mind: Winning the battle in your mind.* Tulsa, OK: Harrison House.

Meyer, J. (2005). *Approval addiction: Overcoming the need to please everyone.* New York, NY: Warner Faith.

Moore, B. (2001). *To live is Christ: Joining Paul's journey of faith.* Nashville, TN: B&H Publishing.

Moore, B. (2007). *Get out of that pit: Straight talk about God's deliverance.* Nashville, TN: Integrity Publishers.

Omartian, S. (2001). *Lord, I want to be whole: The power of prayer and scripture in emotional healing.* Eugene, OR: Harvest House

Omartian, S. (2003). *Lord, I want to be whole: Workbook and journal.* Nashville, TN: Thomas Nelson

Ortberg, J. (2005). *God is closer than you think.* Grand Rapids, MI: Zondervan

Ozrovech, S. (2009). *More than conquerors. 366 devotions.* China: Christian Art Publishers

Robinson, L., Smith, M., & Saisan, J. (2012). *Signs, symptoms, and help for drug problems and substance abuse.* Retrieved from http://helpguide.org/mental/drugsubstanceabuseaddictionsignseffects treatment.htm

Shapiro, R. (2012). *Recovery: The twelve steps as spiritual practice* (2nd ed.). Woodstock, Vermont: Skylight Paths Publishing

Smith, A. (2011). *What women fear: Walking faith the transforms.* Nashville, TN: B&H Publishing Group

Swindoll, C. (2002). *The strength of character.* Nashville, TN: Thomas Nelson, Inc.

Terkeurst, L. (2007). *What happens when women say yes to God: Experiencing life in extraordinary ways.* Eugene, OR: Harvest House Publishers

Thomas, A. (2011). *Choosing joy: A 52-week devotional for discovering happiness.* New York, NY: Howard Brooks

Voskamp, A. (2010). *One thousand gifts.* Grand Rapids, MI: Zondervan

Yeager, K. M. (2012). *Escape from the pit of despair: The journey to improve and maintain your self-esteem.* Bloomington, IN: Crossbooks

AUTHOR BIOGRAPHY

D r. Patricia Allison lives in Goodyear, Arizona, with her husband, Larry, and serves as a professor for Grand Canyon University instructing students who are earning Doctoral degrees in Organizational Leadership. As a university instructor, Dr. Allison specializes in teaching the concepts of servant leadership as modeled by Jesus Christ. Her belief in serving others as Christ served His followers has provided Dr. Allison with a personal drive to emulate the same leadership principles as offered by Christ. Dr. Allison has extensive experience and education in the area of public and private education within urban and inner city environments. Her career has introduced her to many hurting families who struggle daily with poverty, violence, and loss of hope. As a child of divorced parents, Dr. Allison experienced times of personal childhood trauma, giving her an understanding and desire to reach out to others struggling with personal loss and sadness. Her extensive experiences have blessed her with a heart for children living in single parent homes, some of which have been abusive. Additionally, due to these same experiences she has developed a passion for helping women find God's voice in their own lives. Struggling as a teenager to develop a personal relationship with Christ has influenced her decision to dedicate most of her adult life to helping others find God's purpose in their own lives. Dr. Allison has worked with women in a variety of situations, including residential programs, small group settings, and individual mentoring, to help each woman find their path to God's love. Dr. Allison has been blessed to have worked closely with women who have and are experiencing drug addiction, alcoholism, sexual abuse, depression, eating disorders, violence, and many other life altering experiences. She has created a curriculum to be used as a Bible study for women who are searching for inner peace through learning how God can become the light in a world of darkness through His undying love and forgiveness.